ON THE DETECTIVE STORY

EISEN

SERGEI STEIN

On the Detective Story

EDITED AND TRANSLATED BY *Alan Upchurch*

LONDON NEW YORK CALCUTTA

SEAGULL BOOKS, 2017

First published by Seagull Books in 1987

English translation © Seagull Books, 1987

ISBN 978 0 85742 490 7

British Library Cataloguing-in-Publication Data
A catalogue record for this book is available from the British Library

Typeset by Manasij Dutta, Seagull Books, Calcutta, India
Printed and bound in the United States by Maple Press, York, PA
Printed and bound in India by WordsWorth India, New Delhi

CONTENTS

LIST OF ABBREVIATIONS

In the notes, Sergei Eisenstein is referred to as E and the following abbreviations are used for the commonly cited works:

ESW1: Sergei Eisenstein, *Selected Works, Volume 1: Writings, 1922–34* (Richard Taylor ed. and trans.). London: BFI, 1988.

ESW2: Sergei Eisenstein, *Selected Works, Volume 2: Towards a Theory of Montage* (Michael Glenny ed., R. Taylor trans.). London: BFI, 1991.

ESW3: Sergei Eisenstein, *Selected Works, Volume 3: Writings, 1934–47* (Richard Taylor ed., William Powell trans.). London: BFI, 1996.

ESW4: Sergei Eisenstein, *Beyond the Stars: The Memoirs of Sergei Eisenstein* (Richard Taylor ed., William Powell trans.). Calcutta: Seagull Books, 1995.

ER: Richard Taylor (ed.), *The Eisenstein Reader* (Richard Taylor and William Powell trans). London: BFI, 1998.

ERD: Ian Christie and Richard Taylor (eds), *Eisenstein Rediscovered*. London: Routledge, 1993.

FF: Richard Taylor and Ian Christie (eds), *The Film Factory: Russian and Soviet Cinema in Documents, 1896–1939* (Richard Taylor trans.). London: Routledge & Kegan Paul, 1988.

FEL: Sergei Eisenstein, *Film Essays and a Lecture* (Jay Leyda ed. and trans.). Princeton, NJ: Princeton University Press, 1982.

FiFo: Sergei Eisenstein, *Film Form: Essays in Film Theory*, (Jay Leyda ed. and trans.). New York: Harcourt, Brace Jovanovich, 1949.

FS: Sergei Eisenstein, *The Film Sense* (Jay Leyda ed. and trans.). New York: Harcourt, Brace Jovanovich, 1942.

IP: *Izbrannye proizvedeniia v shesti tomakh* [Selected Works in Six Volumes] (S. I. Iutkevich et al. eds). Moscow: Iskusstvo, 1964–71.

NIN: Sergei Eisenstein, *Nonindifferent Nature: Film and the Structure of Things* (Herbert Marshall ed. and trans.). Cambridge: Cambridge University Press, 1987.

RGALI: Rossiiskii gosudarstvennyi arkhiv literatury i iskusstv [Russian State Archive for Literature and the Arts], Moscow.

VGIK: Vsesoiuznyi gosudarstvennyi institut kinmetao-grafii [All-Union State Cinema Institute], Moscow.

THE PSYCHOLOGY OF ART[1]

1 December 1940

Begin by saying that the most interesting problem in the psychology of art—

is neither theme nor content, but how this theme or content becomes, from an object of reality—an object of art.

How an 'event' becomes a 'work'.

What constitutes the process of this transformation from a fact of life into a fact of art?

What is the mystery of the method of art? What is the mystery of so-called form, which distinguishes a phenomenon from its representation in a work of art?

And a second question: where does the attendant affectiveness of art come from?

The primal roots of this affectiveness.

Its meaning.

And, hence, the eternal tendency of art and something accompanying it which is *greater than* emotionality.

23 December 1940

There are many possible problems.

Of psychology as well:

why one does,

what one represents,

how one *ideologically* treats his subject, etc.

Much had been written about all this.

And there is not enough space here for it all.

We shall therefore restrict ourselves to one part.

The part that has been the least understood and described: *method of art*.

That mysterious process in which a phenomenon of nature becomes a fact of art.

And how the very same content crosses over from forms of existence in nature to existence in forms of art.

Goethe addressed this question succinctly and quite categorically . . .[2]

Our art criticism has already contributed quite a bit to this question, although a little of it has been widely published.

It has only been in our own period of the history of the arts that three unprecedented factors, unavailable to earlier stages, have appeared as prerequisites to a clarification of this question.

The method of Marxism-Leninism, which cultivates within us a dialectical examination of phenomena.

Our social structure—a class-free society which the whole history of mankind has not known since the moment its pre-class structure ended at the dawn of primitive society.

Its reflection in superstructures quite naturally also provided models that had never before existed in either creative practice, or in theoretical cognition. Hence a new, never-before-existing course of thought in the realm of artistic activity and the formulation of problems within it.

And this course of thought is immediately armed with the most complete and refined stage of development of the arts, the most complete instrument of art—the cinema which, unlike in other countries—only among us becomes 'the most important of all the arts' (Lenin),[3] the leading art, and wins brilliant victories for the young *Soviet* artistic culture.

In terms of its stage of development, cinema is not only most advanced of the arts in all aspects; it is also like a realization of the 'ideal' to which each of them has individually aspired over the course of the centuries.

Truly:

movement here is alphabetical:

the dynamics of colour—colour cinema,

space—stereometry;

theatre—

close-up and undertone,

transfer through time and space,

10, 20, or 100 sets in a flash;

music—with all its qualities, and concreteness as well etc.

Moreover: cinema is the most modern form of an organic synthesis of art.

Therefore, on the organism of cinema, on its method—there stands out in maximum relief and at the very highest stage of development, the method of art in general. Here it comes out into the open. Here it is analysable and graspable.

And from the heights of this stage of development, in retrospect become comprehensible the 'secret springs' of the structure and method of the individual arts, which seem to converge like streams in the method of cinema.

The method of cinema is like a magnifying glass, through which the method of each of them is visible, and the method of all of them taken together is the fundamental method of every art.

Unarmed with the method of Marxism–Leninism,

without our present stage of social development

and, finally, without this still so little used marvel of human genius and technology—the cinema—we could never peer with such dissecting precision into the most secret organism of form.

••

An event in nature and an event in a work of art are somehow different. In what way?

On a certain battleship in 1905, a mutiny broke out over some maggoty meat. A doctor pronounced it edible. And when the uprising broke out, for that very reason he was one of the first, along with the hateful officers, to go flying overboard.

But at one point it became necessary to remind the viewer that the doctor had been abolished.

What could be simpler? A wave rolls in to the shore and carries out the body of the drowned doctor.

'Meanwhile . . .'—as they loved to write in intertitles in the old silent cinema—instead of this, the director did something completely different.

On a hawser of the battleship dangles . . . pince-nez.[4]

An effect a hundred times greater. Popularity.

An old king loses his mind. He has imprudently divided up his kingdom between his daughters.

He wanders homeless in a field.

Anger and the fury of outraged emotions storm within him. The landscape, it would seem, should have nothing to do with it. Fury can rage in a field, in a house, in rain and in warm weather. But for some reason, the dramatist—Shakespeare—compels the elements to howl with equal rage and in tone to King Lear's fury: Lear's wailing blends with the howling of a storm.

And the effect from this blending of the emotion of the unhappy king with the 'emotion' of the elements, helps make this scene one of the most remarkable in world drama ...

The ruthless clique of Wall Street, the insoluble contradictions of the bourgeois system. The law of capitalism destroys farmers. Drives them from their leased land. Their equipment, personal belongings and horses are sold for almost nothing. Newspapers are full of it. They move most deeply those who are directly affected (Goethe's 'wer etwas dazu zu tun hat' [whoever has anything to do with it]).

But when the real-life sorrow of a farmer selling his horses enters the sphere of artistic treatment—it becomes a pathetic monologue in the hands of the excellent writer Steinbeck and from the pages of one of the most powerful novels of recent years—from the pages of *The Grapes of Wrath*—it suddenly sounds as follows (but say it any other way—and 75 per cent of its ability to grip will be lost):[5]

Now, what'll you give for the team and wagon? Those fine bays, matched they are, matched in colour, matched the way they walk, stride to stride. In the stiff pull—straining hams and buttocks, split-second timed together. And in the morning, the light on them, bay light. They look over the fence sniffing for us, and the stiff ears swivel to hear us, and the black forelocks! I've got a girl. She likes to braid the manes and forelocks, puts little red bows on them. Likes to do it. Not any more. I could tell you a funny story about that girl and that off bay. Would make you laugh. Off horse is eight, near is ten, might have been twin colts the way they work together. See? The teeth. Sound all over. Deep lungs. Feet fair and clean. How much? Ten dollars? For both? And the wagon—Oh, Jesus Christ! I'd shoot 'em for dog feed first. Oh, take 'em! Take 'em quick, mister. You're buying a little girl plaiting the forelocks, taking off her hair ribbon to make bows, standing back, head cocked, rubbing the soft noses with her cheek. You're buying years of work, toil in the sun; you're buying a sorrow that can't talk. But watch it, mister. There's a premium goes with this pile of junk and the bay horses—so beautiful—a packet of bitterness to grow in your house and to flower, some day . . . [6]

The fine old Russian classic, Gogol, writes of Taras Bulba: 'Bulba shrugged his shoulders and rode off for his detachment.'

Then he corrects his manuscript and the final version of the text suddenly comes out sounding: 'Shrugging his shoulders, Taras Bulba marvelled at the spontaneous resourcefulness of the Jewish character, and rode off for the camp.'[7]

Another—Pushkin—sketches a Ukrainian night. A night like any other.

The night of the Ukraine is still,
The skies alive with starry glitter.
The drowsy ether lacks the will
To shake its languor; barely twitter
The poplar twigs with silver gleams.

But then the dispassionate description is dramatized: filled with dark thoughts and remorse, Mazepa steps into the scene, and this same landscape starts to behave quite differently:

Distraught, oppressed by haunting dreams,
Mazepa roams; the starry skies—
A million marking, noting eyes—
Pursue him with their mocking stares;
The poplars in their swaying pairs
Are lisping, bowing to their sisters
Like justices exchanging whispers.
The summer's dim nocturnal spell
Hangs airless, like a dungeon cell.[8]

Tolstoy wanted to condemn ownership. So condemn it, would be thing one. But that is not enough for him. He creates an image of an honourable, hard-working horse—Kholstomer, meditates his character, invents speech for him. And at night among the other horses, he causes him to share the following words on this theme:

> Men rule in life, not by deeds, but by words. They love not so much the possibility of doing or not doing anything, as the possibility of talking about different objects in words agreed on between them. Such words, considered very important among them, are the words, *my, mine, ours,* which they employ for various things, beings, and objects; even for the earth, people, and horses ... And men struggle in life not to do what they consider good, but to call as many things as possible their own.
>
> I am convinced now that herein lies the substantial difference between men and us.[9]

And in reading Tolstoy, Pushkin, Gogol, Steinbeck, in watching *Lear, Potemkin*, or any other picture capable of competently presenting a so-called 'close-up', the reader and viewer experience a quite special emotionally-sensuous state.

And a film or stage director, or a writer, knows just as firmly that should he write or depict the same thing by means other than this special method—even while keeping the same content—the very 'magic' of the gripping affectiveness will slip away from the work like smoke . . .

What have the writer, dramatist and director done?

For the purpose of achieving a heightened, not an informational, not only cognitive, but emotionally gripping effect, they did the following:

They first, at the necessary moment, discarded the whole (the doctor) and in its place presented a part (the pince-nez).

They second compelled the entire surroundings of a man (Lear) to take on the form of that man's state (the storm).

They third equated an object of actual trade with an invisible object —labour.

They fourth made a slight rearrangement of words, switching the positions of the predicate and subject, i.e. mentioning the fact of movement before describing *who* moves (Taras).

They fifth took the quiet phenomena of nature (stars, poplars) and personified them—one he made whispering judges (the poplars), the other he compelled to wink or stare with fixed reproach (the stars) at the accused.

Finally, they sixth took ordinary, fine Russian words, stripped away the relative meaning given them by an exploitative society over the centuries, and gave them back their original form of a concrete, objective fact (Communion).[10]

Where there is absolutely no underlying natural fact, as in ownership—which contradicts the organic world— nothing is left. 'Any and all masks' were stripped away from the idol of bourgeois society—'ownership', under which not even a 'naked king' was left standing! At the same time, he also humanized an old horse.

And a second question—did they do something different or something identical, if not in deed, then in method?

And might this method conceal the very same thing which also lies at the heart of the method of transforming a fact of reality into a fact of art?

For this, let's see what we are reminded of by the harmony into which our author, director, and dramatist transferred the material of their content.

Let's add to them yet one more figure—a composer who dreamed of a certain . . . synthesis of the arts as the basis for a type of spectacle never before seen—a musical drama, which was supposed to replace opera.

And here we shall take the liberty of disturbing the ghost of the great Wagner, because a certain Max Nordau in his book, *Entartung* [Degeneration], slung against him in a polemical fervour the very words which could lead to the key (a one-sided, false key, as we shall see below), where the means ought to be sought of the 'method' of everything that the aforementioned authors did—each in his own way, but taken all together, in the spirit of one and the same phenomenon, having an absolutely accurate address.

And, although the deciphering of the true picture of this situation came from a totally different realm—the realm of experimental composition in cinema[11]—for the soundness of our argument, this attack on Wagner by Max Nordau is very appropriate for us here—Max Nordau, who, for as much as he perceived, overlooked just as much in the phenomenon that was accomplished in the formation of Wagner's programme:

> The effort to return to beginnings is, however, a peculiarity of degeneration, and founded in its deepest essence ... Wagner's fusion of the arts is a pendant to this notion. His *Artwork of the Future* is the artwork of times long past. What he takes for evolution is retrogression, and a return to a primeval human, nay, to a pre-human stage.[12]

'But he's right!—explodes from those reading this excerpt.

Right or wrong, how and why—we don't yet know.

But it really does seem so.

And perhaps the same principle also underlies the six examples, drawn at random from the method of art, which we cited above.

The humanized horse and . . . totemism.[13]

The poplars and stars and . . . animism.

Where else have we encountered the same description? In Engels, of course![14]

For don't we know of lionesses, etc.?[15]

Have we not heard of childbirth and gates . . . and how *öliges* [oiliness] is not allowed when someone is hunting (Lear)?[16]

Doesn't the bear's tooth also belong here?—*pars pro toto*.[17]

But all this is far from being facts of an uncoordinated nature—these facts all belong to an absolutely specific complex of phenomena.

Complex, diffuse, i.e. *primitive* mentality.

Moreover, they also belong to those mental states which either phylogenetically repeat them (in the mentality of the child), or which—in pathological phe-nomena—regress to it (dreams, narcosis, schizophrenia).

'But come now, is this true, can this really be?!'

Let's work . . . backwards. Let's draw two or three traits from the fund familiar to us and see if we can find a corresponding 'analogy' to them in the methodology of art.

Let's take what would seem to be the most unlikely case:

Bororo, Birman, Davydov.[18]

The *Fehlhandlung* [accidental action] (Kretschmer's chicken) and the technique of the stage, the play.[19]

Primal rhythmicality and the rhythmization indispen-sable in an affect.[20]

..

Stop joking! What—do you mean to say that the method of art is a reversion of our enlightened, modern intellect to the twilight stage of primitive thought? You want to put this great, cultural activity which 'deceptively elevates us' on the same level with narcosis, dreaming, schi-zo-phre-ni-a!

Stop it, stop it! If we were Max Nordau, that's what we would do, and we would go even one step further: we would abolish art.

But Nordau saw only one side of the phenomenon. Dialectics teaches us to look at a phenomenon from all sides and as a whole. It is then that a quite different picture is revealed for art, than for possible or impossible analogies, reminiscent realms, etc.

What takes place in art.[21]

Social mobility at the top.

Can we, however, imagine a realm of art where truly only one generatrix could be found, the 'lowest' one, for example?

Its characteristic feature would be an almost total *invariability* of this art from ancient times to the very present, almost disregarding countries, epochs and nations that have outworn their primitive appearance, and which would *interest and excite outside of* and *without* any content. That sounds unlikely. But such a variety (true, extremely marginal) among the arts is to be found, such a spectacle exists.

People go to it by the thousands breathlessly to watch a man place a chair on top of so many chairs, and these on so many tables, and standing tiptoe on the mouth of the bottle placed on the leg of the highest upside-down chair, try to keep his balance; to watch him catch his balance as he stands motionless with an umbrella or glides quickly along a tightrope. This game of purposely lost and regained balance elicits squeals of delight.

And then these same thousands watch a 'magus' or magician pull from his sleeve, one after another, handkerchiefs, live piglets, doves, a cup of water, a glowing light bulb, a live hare ...

The programme is concluded by a man in a colourful jacket, who, before the very eyes of his highly esteemed public, tames and 'domesticates' a whole pack of ferociously roaring tigers, lions and polar bears ...

Page through the history of circuses—it has always been like this. Page through the history of the Soviet circus since 1917, and you will see that it couldn't be otherwise: all attempts to 'politicize' the circus, to give meaning to it, to make it topical, to enrich it with new, untraditional numbers—have led to naught. (Only clowns acts and satirical ballads, and then in a very superficial form on a terribly low level, are occasionally topical.)

Drivers 'fly' from trapeze to trapeze.

Horses and elephants submit on their knees to the will of man, 'humanized' orang-utans walk, small dogs in human costumes act out a melodrama and, whining in a childish falsetto, the red-haired clown demonstrates his simple and ever-infantile pranks to the howling of children and grown-ups, carefree and serious, fathers of families (!)

and bookkeepers (!), foremen (!) and professors (!), all laughing at the same thing, with the laughter of their grandfathers, great-grand-fathers and ancestors!

What causes people to throng to the circus every night all over the globe? The three-ring Barnums in America, the winter circuses in winter, the travelling tent tops in summer?

What compels the 'grey-haired veteran' to watch so intensely the high-wire artiste lose and catch his balance?

Why is the serious man in glasses pleased at the sight of a duel of wills between a man and a panther? Why do his eyes sparkle with pride when the panther sprawls before its master and sovereign, submits at his feet like an obedient kitten?

Why is the top-notch accountant fascinated by ducks, hares, and hens jumping out of a farcical magician's top hat, even though he knows fully well that all this is sleight of hand and not the slightest swindle?

It takes but a moment's reflections to see that the point here is not at all nonsense. For that which the viewer sees before him in the arena—is a millionth variant of reconstruction of the same thing he himself went through long, long ago in the form of his ancestors. The magus-shaman was only quite recently banished by Soviet power from the customs of the outlying regions of our country. Even today we are stirred by magnificent pictures of struggle between the Dzhigit horseman and the wild steppe horse, submitting to the will of man.[22]

And each of us recalls, if not with his head and memory, then with his aural labyrinth and once bruised elbows and knees, that difficult period of childhood, when almost the sole content in the struggle for a place under the sun for each of us as a child was the problem of balance during the transition from the four-legged standing of a 'toddler' to the proud two-legged standing of the master of the universe. An echo of the child's personal biography, of the centuries past of his entire species and kind.

'Is it a pleasant memory?'—is this the fascination of this spectacle, if we extend the concept of memory far beyond the sphere of consciously registered sensations to sensations merely sensuously experienced?

I don't think so. Even less, the rather vulgar in itself and even more vulgarized idea of compensation or reaction of the suppressed. No, more likely what we have here is an artificial return to the psychological *habitus*, corresponding to the stage of a similar type of *activity*.

If this circle of activities leads the viewer into the intellectual structure of a certain level with the same activity, then the same thing is accomplished more subtly by any part by a more subtle method. Developing step by step a prescription of sensuous thought in elements of the structure form, they lead the viewer to the level of the psychological structure which corresponds to the social structure for which such thought was typical and characteristic, for it too is reflected in the methods of the functioning of this consciousness.

And that is the most remarkable part of all. For the composition of the elements of sensuous thought is not some 'pre-biological' or 'God-given', 'twilight' subconsciousness; it is the very same consciousness, only reflecting a different social stage of development, and therefore a completely different one structurally.

And the reproduction of the norms of the thinking and behaviour, characteristic of sensuous consciousness, evokes sensations related not to the social structure in which the viewer now exists, but to the one during which thinking took shape and arose according to such norms and forms . . .

But what was this [social] structure during which consciousness—still sensuous, not yet artificially splitting emotionality and cognition—took shape in precisely such norms?

Primitive society. The tribal structure . . .

This will tell us very little unless we recall the basic, chief, social characteristic of this structure. The characteristic which sets it beyond comparison with all other epochs and successive generations ...

This characteristic is eloquently noted and characterized in the cornerstone doctrine of Marx–Engels–Lenin—*The Communist Manifesto*.[23]

And thus, echoing the prescription of form, each of us psychologically inculcates himself into a type of consciousness that knows no yoke of class character in its creation and definition.

Form permits us to experience it.

The form in any given work at any given moment permits the realization of the age-old nostalgia that was expressed by Morgan:

> Democracy in government, brotherhood in society, equality in rights and privileges, and universal education, foreshadow the next higher plane of society to which experience, intelligence and knowledge are steadily tending. It will be a revival, in a higher form, of the liberty, equality and fraternity of the ancient gentes.[24]

Form always appeals to the Golden Age of human existence.

Even an approximation of this stage of the cradle—the stage of childhood—already radiates with incomprehensible attractiveness.

Marx on antiquity.[25]

This is even more deeply rooted, purer, and closer.

But there is a characteristic difference.

The stage of childhood presents antiquity objectively, substantially representationally, narratively and thematically at the threshold of the initial source.

Still deeper—outward appearance disappears and structure remains. Structure and method fascinate. But therefore, they are also pervasive—not bound by epoch (like antiquity), but universal, as universal as the method of metaphor or synecdoche—as a method of invariables from Homer to Mayakovsky,[26] and as a form of expression equally dear to Pushkin and the Aztec, but in terms of their content, incommensurable from year to year, from epoch to epoch, from class to class, and from individual to individual, each reflecting and refracting social reality in his own way through his own individuality within the collective, through his simultaneously class-bound and singular consciousness.

And here we come to the second most important point concerning the basic ideas expounded here.

The palette of the means of form is limitless. The master has a choice of *pars pro toto*, concrete thinking, personification, rhythmization, and what not! To a certain extent and at a certain point, they are present as a large or small conglomerate in every artistic action and act, in all epochs, among all nationalities, in the creative work of every master. But then at some period of art, all elements start to move as if towards a focal point—towards one certain feature; the others seem to fade into the background—one certain 'characteristic' trait moves out in front.

It becomes the leading one.

But a trait is usually not confined to any one specific, single realm of art, but, belonging first and foremost to the whole mentality of a certain epoch, equally underlies all its manifestations. And art starts to bear its specific, distinguishing mark of style—a 'paltryism' if it is insignificant (Cubism, Futurism, Tactilism, Dadaism, Surrealism, etc.), in contrast to such 'fundamentalisms' as, for example, realism!

Being a function of selection of socially conditioned thinking, *this or that* tendency in the choice of leading methodical features from the general fund of certain elements, is no longer *universal*, no longer accidental, no longer neutral, but is profoundly socially conditioned, for such, too, is the mentality that produces the selection.

It by no means functions according to principles of 'prescription writing', assigning the leading role to this or that paragraph from the fund of sensuous thought. The prophets and proselytes of such tendencies are usually very poorly versed in this realm and, in fact, this realm itself has not stood and does not stand in such close connection with the method of art.

Nonetheless, every trend usually has a very emphatic, militant programme. This programme—once stripped of this or that literary clothing—usually always betrays the branch within sensuous thought, upon which it intends to build its trend.

Incidentally, even one and the same trait from this fund in the hands of artists of different epochs, different social moulds and different individualities—allows for the finest nuances within the same feature.[27]

[There is nothing urban in Tolstoy's passing scenery, neither in the people nor the objects he describes—everything in Tolstoy is rural, mainly peasants and landowners. If a merchant in a caftan should walk along the road, he would not even notice him, but if he did, he would not bother with a description. The characters in Tolstoy's landscape are pilgrims, i.e. the same peasant women, coachmen, carters, the same muzhiks and horses. In Gogol, there is an abundance of urban and residential structures and then,

in the distance, a landowner's house; and what is significant for Gogol is that there is nothing separating the property line from the human line except a comma—they move
as one: 'whether a market, or some neighbouring dandy
come to town—nothing was lost upon my fresh and keen
mind'; and jars of stale sweets on shelves stand in the same
line with an infantry officer and a merchant and a local
official (people are equal to things, and vice versa). In
Gogol's landscape there is a landowner's house and a garden, and in projection, the landowner himself with his
family. Here, the resemblance between their passing motifs
is at its fullest, but again what a difference for all the sim-
ilarity . . .

For greater clarity, let us recite these passages:

Gogol

When nearing some landowner's village, I used to
eye with curiosity the tall, narrow, wooden belfry
or the dark and spacious outlines of the old
wooden church. From afar, through the green
foliage, the red roof and the white chimneys of the
landowner's house beckoned me enticingly, and I
waited impatiently until the gardens which shaded
it on both sides would part and reveal its then—
alas, then!—by no means vulgar appearance; and
from it I tried to guess what sort of a person the

landowner was, whether he was stout, whether he had sons or a full complement of six daughters with laughing girlish voices, games and, as always, the youngest a beauty, whether they all had black eyes, and whether the old man was of a hearty disposition or as brooding as the last days of September when he consulted the calendar and bored the young folk with talk of rye and wheat.[28]

Tolstoy

Yonder, far beyond the ravine, a village church with its green roof is visible against the bright blue sky; yonder is a hamlet, the red roof of a gentle-man's house, and a green garden. Who lives in this house? Are there children in it, father, mother, tutor? Why should we not go to this house, and make the acquaintance of the owner?][29]

Let's take at random a few theses from the programme of 'isms' belonging to the period of disintegration of bourgeois society: Cubism Tactilism, Surrealism.

As to their existence before they were such, they them-selves as 'styles' were a hypertrophy of *pars* at the expense of *toto*, i.e. everything which in a normally realistic work participates in a unity, is here dismembered into particu-lars, each of which stands in opposition to the whole.

Pars pro toto in realism.

Pars pro toto in impressionism.

(The naturalism of Zola as impressionism in its non-generalizing and disconnected instantaneousness of a *particular* detail. According to Hamann.)[30]

Pars pro toto in other 'isms'.

If such is the case in entire, sometimes quite major, 'trends' as impressionism, for example, then it is precisely the same within the 'style', 'manner'', 'tendency', 'handwriting', and 'method', of a single author.

Ausblick für uns. [The outlook for us.]

The future does not need to be predicted.

It is right here with us. Coming into being. Being born. Being made. It is presently a matter that is in our hands. But already it is starting to work in reverse. It is breaking into the sphere of relations. Problems of consciousness. Morals. Ethics. Activity. The superstructures are cracking. The new. The unprecedented. Classlessness is entering into them.

NOTES

1 This section contains notes on the psychology of art begun on 25 November 1940 by E at the request of Alexander R. Luria (1902–77), the Soviet psychologist and pioneer of neuropsychology (see also *ESW4*, p. 611). In November 1947, Luria asked E to deliver a series of lectures on the subject. He was prevented from doing so by his death in February 1948. This translation of 'The Psychology of Art' and that of the subsequent 'Conspectus' was made by Alan Upchurch from the Russian text first published in *Psikhologiia protsessov khudozhestvennogo tvorchestva* [The Psychology of the Processes of Artistic Creation] (Leningrad: Nauka, 1980). Most of the notes to that Soviet edition, by Naum Kleiman and Tatiana Drozhzhina, have been translated here as well. Archival references have been omitted but the interested reader can find them in the above edition.

2 There is a gap in the manuscript here and the quotation that E had in mind has not been identified.

3 This quotation was attributed to Lenin by Anatoli V. Lunacharsky (1875–1933), People's Commissar for Enlightenment from 1917 to 1929, to a conversation

between the two in 1922 recalled only after Lenin's death in January 1924. See *FF*, pp. 56–7.

4 The allusion is of course to E's own *Bronenosets Potemkin* [The Battleship Potemkin, 1925].

5 John Steinbeck (1902–68), American novelist, published *The Grapes of Wrath*, a sympathetic and realistic portrayal of the plight of migrant agricultural workers in California, in 1939. It was immediately made into a film directed by John Ford, starring Henry Fonda, and released in January 1940.

6 John Steinbeck, *The Grapes of Wrath* (New York: Viking, 1939), p. 89.

7 E borrows his example from: I. E. Mandel'shtam, *O kharaktere gogolevskago stilia* [On the Character of Gogol's Style] (St Petersburg: n.p., 1902), p. 118. He used the same source and example in his first speech to the All-Union Creative Conference of Soviet Film-makers, in January 1935, *ESW3*, pp. 34–5.

8 Alexander Pushkin, 'Poltava' in *Pushkin: Collected Narrative and Lyrical Poetry* (W. Arndt trans.) (Ann Arbor, MI: Ardis, 1984), p. 348.

9 Leo Tolstoy, 'Kholstomer' in *The Novels and Other Works*, VOL. 12: *The Insider and Other Stories* (E. Hapgood trans.) (New York: Scribner's, 1913).

10 Apparently E intended to compare Tolstoy's story with the Christian ritual of Communion, in which the believer symbolically 'incorporates' the spirit of Christ by 'partaking' of His body (bread) and blood (wine). In a later note E suggests that both are illustrations of a primitive belief in totemism.

11 E has in mind his own attempts in *Oktiabr* [October, 1927] and *General'naia liniia* [The General Line, released as *Staroe i novoe* (The Old and the New), 1929] to elicit 'sensuous' reactions in the audience through calculated montage constructs. See 'The Dramaturgy of Film Form', *ESW1*, pp. 151–60; *ER*, pp. 93–110; translated as 'A Dialectic Approach to Film Form', *FiFo*, pp. 45–63; and 'The Fourth Dimension in Cinema', *ESW1*, pp. 181–94, partially translated as 'Methods of Montage', *FiFo*, pp. 72–83.

12 Max Nordau, *Degeneration* (New York: Appleton, 1895), p. 176.

13 E's manuscript contains the following unfinished note in the margin: 'A description of Communion and ... for don't we know (an example of concrete thought) ...'

14 The citation E had in mind has not been identified.

15 E's manuscript contains the following note: '[In reference] to Steinbeck: A lioness carries her cub *around the cage*, believing that she is as far away from the starting point as the distance she covered while circling the same spot.' E apparently intended to compare this with the 'primitivism' that allows Steinbeck's farmer to equate his horses with years of work.

16 Cf. *ESW3*, p. 31, *FiFo*, pp. 134–5.

17 Cf. the analysis of the pince-nez episode in *ESW3*, p. 30; *FiFo*, pp. 132–3.

18 The instance of the Bororo and their identification with red parakeets is also discussed in *ESW3*, p. 32, *FiFo*, pp. 135–6, as well as in *On Disney*.

Serafima G. Birman (1890-1976) was later to play the part of Efrosinia Staritskaia in *Ivan the Terrible*. Cf. *ESW3*, p. 33; *FiFo*, pp. 136–7.

The example E had in mind from the career of the actor Vladimir N. Davydov (1849–1925) has not been determined.

19 E returned to this question in his January 1948 article, 'Towards the Question of *Mise-en-scène*', published for the first time in its entirety in: *Eisenstein: Le Mouvement de l'art* (F. Albera and N. Kleiman eds) (Paris: Editions du Cerf, 1986). He begins the section '*Mise en jeu*' and '*Mise en geste*' (pp. 179–80):

> Sigmund Freud, in his time, caused quite a stir when he announced (proving and substantiating) that the slip of the tongue and the *Fehlhandlung* [accidental action] are actually not a slip of the tongue or *Fehlhandlung*, but are the true intentions breaking through the *Deckhandlung* [masking action], by means of which they are concealed, hidden or 'suppressed', owing to external conditions, necessities and circumstances.
>
> It was in this context that Konstantin Sergeyevich [Stanislavsky] promoted the 'subtext' as the current of a speech's true content, parallel to the superficially conventional course of dialogue: the true line of content under the cover of absolute appearance . . . But this phenomenon should concern, not only the realm of mental content and hence the content of the actor's actions, but the whole plastic-spatial and aural expression

(embodiment) of acting, as well as all elements of the spectacle as a whole.

In his unfinished book, *Method* [1940–48, first volume published, Moscow, 2002], E discussed the same example with reference to the chapter 'The Motor Storm' from E. Kretschmer, *A Text-Book of Medical Psychology* (London: Oxford University Press, 1934), p. 117:

> The most striking example of an atavistic motor storm is the hysterical attack which, in addition to a wealth of rhythmical elements (tremors and convulsions), releases a welter of the most violent movements representing both defence and rapture with powerful participation of vegetative and reflex mechanisms . . . [The hysterical woman] will not think things over and arrive at a clear decision as to her situation and the best way out of her difficulty. She will work herself up into an undifferentiated, oppressive, but very strong state of emotion which is experienced as a general feeling that everything is unbearable and that she must break away at all costs. This state of emotional tension finds relief, without any antecedent motivated deliberation, in tempestuous motor discharge, exactly as in the case of the infusoria, the trapped mouse or bird. A scared chicken in an enclosed space cackles, flutters, and struggles until this superabundance of motor activities eventually brings it to a hole in the fence through which it can escape.

20 In a section of *Method* entitled 'The Rhythmic Drum',
E analyses methods of:

cultivation undergone primarily by a man who
is 'doomed' to enter the circle of sensuous
thought . . . The first means possessed by this
cultivation is that which might be called a
'rhythmic drum'. . . Starting with the simplest
and most literal—the ritual drums of the
voodoo cult (in Cuba). Their measured
beating, in a continuously accelerating tempo,
leads the responsive listeners into a state of
total frenzy. And they are totally in the power
of the images flashing through their excited
imagination, or of whatever their leader suggests to them . . . The rhythmic drum of the
Catholic religious machine is described by
Zola in *Lourdes* . . . For Orthodox ecstasy—
Gorky has left a description . . . In short—the
answer to a natural question: why does a
rhythmic drum thus return us to regressive
stages of thought? The answer suggests itself
if we recall that everything in us that occurs
apart from consciousness and will—occurs
rhythmically: the beating of the heart and
breathing, peristalsis of the intestines, merger
and separation of cells, etc. Switching off
consciousness, we sink into the inviolable
rhythm of breathing during sleep, the rhythm
of sleepwalking etc. And conversely—the
monotony of a repeated rhythm brings us
closer to those states 'next to consciousness',

where only the traits of sensuous thought are capable of functioning fully.

21 Cf. *ESW3*, p. 38; *FiFo*, pp. 144–5.

22 The magus-shaman played a significant part in the customs of Siberia and the Soviet Far East. The Dzhigit horsemen came from the Transcaucasian and Central Asian republics and were famed for their daring, acrobatic riding skill. They have long been an act in the Russian and Soviet circus.

23 There is a gap in the manuscript here and the precise quotation E intended to use has not been identified.

24 L. H. Morgan, *Ancient Society; Or, Researches in the Lines of Human Progress from Savagery through Barbarism to Civilization* (New York: Henry Holt, 1878), p. 552.

25 E has in mind the following passage from: Karl Marx, 'Introduction to a Critique of Political Economy' in Karl Marx and Friedrich Engels, *The German Ideology* (C. J. Arthur ed.) (New York: International Publishers, 1981), pp. 150–1:

> An adult cannot become a child again, or he becomes childish. But does the naiveté of the child not give him pleasure, and does not he himself endeavour to reproduce the child's veracity on a higher level? Does not in every epoch the child represent the character of the period in its natural veracity? Why should not the historical childhood of humanity, where it attained its most beautiful form, exert an eternal charm because it is a stage that will never recur? There are rude children and precocious children. Many of the ancient peoples belong

to this category. The Greeks were normal children. The charm their art has for us does not conflict with the immature stage of the society in which it originated. On the contrary its charm is a consequence of this and is inseparably linked with the fact that the immature social conditions which gave rise, and which alone could give rise, to this art cannot recur.

26 Vladimir V. Mayakovsky (1893–1930), Soviet poet and playwright.

27 E left a gap here in the manuscript with a note: 'Gogol—Tolstoy (in Myshkovskaya)'. He apparently intended to cite the section that follows in square brackets from L. M. Myshkovskaia, *L. Tolstoi: rabota i stil* (Moscow: Sovetskii pisatel, 1938), pp. 91–2.

28 Nikolai V. Gogol, *Dead Souls* (G. Reavey trans.) (Oxford: Oxford University Press, 1957), pp. 129–30.

29 Leo Tolstoy, *The Novels and Other Works*, VOL. 10: *Childhood, Boyhood, Youth* (E. Hapgood trans.) (New York: Scribner's, 1913), p. 119.

30 R. Hamann, *Der Impressionismus in Leben und Kunst* [Impressionism in Life and Art] (Cologne: Dumont-Schauberg, 1907).

CONSPECTUS OF LECTURES ON THE PSYCHOLOGY OF ART

19 November 1947

Alexander Luria telephoned yesterday, inviting me to give a series of lectures on the psychology of art at the Psychology Institute of Moscow University (for students in the senior class).

Not yet having made up my mind to do it, I naturally started planning this morning while in bed how I would present such a series.

For the hundredth time, I arranged and put in order several themes; basically, the transition from expressive movement to an image in a work of art, which is the same thing transposed from the vehicle (the author) to the material; material into which the inner stage of expressive movement is inserted—not as a motor process, but as the process of interaction between layers of consciousness. For the development of this argument, see the appendix.

But here is the most important point:

It only just dawned on me that what I have been concerned with these past few days—thinking about how to write a history of cinema—fits entirely within the system of this conception of mine.

A conception which dates, however, from 1920.

1920-1925: in the realm of expressive movement (the theatre)

1925-1935: in the realm of the image (*For a Great Cinema Art*).[1]

1935-1948: in cinema.

1948—as the principle of the history of cinema.

Truly, my formula:

(1) of the newsreel as the cradle of cinema (with a digression on the question that here the ornament, ᎧᎧᎧ, is representational art);

(2) of the newsreel as a component of the film-process of imagistic (artistic) cinema (especially at its origins and now—in a new quality—at the end of the first thirty years);

(3) of the organic link between these forms over the course of history—and a new aspect resulting from new material in the form of art yet one more avatar of the formula of interaction between the direct and the mediated source.[2]

Their conflict (with Engels' adjustment of 'the struggle for life' in *Dialectics of Nature*);[3] as the basis of expressive movement (an image of expression and a distortion of the body in the process of interaction between both sources);[4] as the basis of an artistic image (as the interaction between the sources of sensuous, pre-logical thought and logical thought);

and it also underlies:

the interaction between a direct copy of phenomenon (an *automatic* 'imprint') in the newsreel and a mediation ('how the shot is *cut*,' i.e. what is selected from the phenomenon and how the selection is *compared*, i.e. montage: *a conscious selection* and comparison). Resulting in the process of an image coming into being through the interaction of both.

(In different phases of development—an emphasis on different points of the process.)

Cinema becomes the third block in the general system.

It is interesting that in cinema this outline is visible in historical (concrete) evolution from its origins to our thirty-year anniversary[5]—in its stylistic varieties.

Thus both as a corroboration of the whole system, and as the taking of an extra-historicality from it (supposedly capable of being recognized underneath).

And forming at the same time a *three-part basis* of the first volume of *the history of cinema*:

1. Expressive man.
2. The artistic image. } excellent.
3. The art of cinema.

We practitioners have to be able to depict expressive behaviour of people and to create (impressive) expressive, artistic images in any given circumstances through any character.

Expressive—*striking*—affective.

But only that which proceeds in accordance with laws of nature can affect.

(This is also true for an actor: he is effective only if the movements of his body and soul, performed on the stage, evolve in accordance with the laws of human conduct.

And also for the imagistic structure of a work, which must copy the structure of the process by which imagistic concepts arise and exist within us, and in which our feelings and thoughts converge.)

Hence the necessity to know what these laws are.

A materialist approach instead of a mystic veil covering the phenomena of expression and creative work.

Two levels of examination: expressive man and an expressive work (an image being its *crux* [kernel]).

••

Expressive man.

Our task, essentially, is to compel a man to behave *without physical reason* as if:

drowning without water, escaping from fire without flames, loving a girl who might be completely hostile to you in real life, dying while remaining alive and so on.

How is this possible?

The warring schools of expressive acting technique.

At the beginning of the Revolution, three lines were drawn.

Today, they are no longer three lines, but three different approaches to one and the same point.

And more precisely—each one enters the total process in its own way and at the right moment.[6]

The task is the same as swallowing a pill.

And again there are three ways of doing this:

1. By drinking a bucket of water (factually washing the pill down with).

2. By touching the lips and tongue with a glass and drop (activating the swallowing motion reflexively).

3. By studying the mechanism of the motion and learning how to do it the same as any other: riding a sled, holding a bow, playing a triad on the piano.

Experiments with embryos.

The eyelid is closed—and the whole figure rolls down.

i.e. an integral reaction in pure form, even with an absence of an impulse transmitted to a particular spot.

In the adult system, from the feet remains, but with a transmission of a stimulus through the *whole* system.[7]

In the embryo, there is not yet a conflicting reaction.

A transition to *form*.

As yet we have said nothing specific about art: we have been speaking about *reconstruction*, the reproduction of a fact—*behaviour in specific circumstances*.

We defined as expressive—expediency in the arrangement of a figure in the process of a specific activity.

The more cleansed of the accidental—the more expressive.

It is then that the meaning of the action can be read—
the content of the action.

Let us move on now from a man's action to the 'general picture' of what takes place (the conditions in which and because of which he acts), and see what is required for the content of this general (dynamic) picture also to be readable.

Le Père Goriot. The arrest of Vautrin.[8]

A wrong solution.

A correct solution. All variations will be based on the same formula: ⌐◌ **— a circle and an outsider.**

Briefly about styles:

from naturalism	⎫	what they practically are,
through realism to	⎬	and why, when and how—
Constructivism	⎭	conditioned by history.

(A very brief *Aussicht* [perspective] on the adjacent.)

And already a method starts to appear; the metaphorical designation should be returned to its underlying dynamic action—a non-metaphorical reading.[9]

'Attachment' and the detective.[10]

For a practical beginning, this is sufficient. But let us look deeper and generalize further.

On the basis of a single circumstance—that the metaphorical must be returned to the non-metaphorical for visual cogency—it is difficult to make a generalization.

Therefore, let's keep searching in concrete examples.

'A man enters through a door' in life and on the stage.

The non-readability and readability of this act on the stage.

'In order for him *noticeably* to enter the door, he must first step away from it and then move through it.' The paradox here is only apparent.

(Demonstrate running joyfully out through a door to greet a visitor off-stage.)

Cite examples from different realms:

as soon as you have a real-life action of labour—the scheme inevitably works as a whole:

try driving a nail without a refusal,

try jumping over a fence without backing up.

From these *necessities*, it is transferred to any reading: a ledge of a cupboard as a 'transfer' from the utilitarian ledge of a house. A cupboard as a little house *en petit*! The abolition of ledges on cupboards occurred after the abolition of ledges in architecture!—Le Corbusier; houses without ledges. A different solution of roofs and house tops. And again this enters metaphorically into a miniature copy of a house in the form of a cupboard. The first (ledge) is less logical than the second, but both are equally reflected in the re-working of their tops. Till an independent, 'non-apish' solution of a cupboard appears, based on its own requirements: a cupboard . . . built into the wall par excellence (see modern houses).

In theatrical technique.

Our seventeenth century, Johann Gregory.[11]

Japanese traditions of the eighteenth century. Kabuki (Sadanji on the *hanamichi*).[12]

Ancient China—Mei Lan-fan.[13]

But also far beyond the bounds of theatre in . . . tactics!

Lenin on a step back, so as to better leap ahead.

Citation.[14]

Something already exceedingly comprehensive.

Let us examine the formula itself:

life: $A \longrightarrow B$

art: $C \underset{A}{\overset{\longrightarrow}{\longleftarrow}} B$

What the second turns out to be is not an affirmation, but a negation of a negation, i.e. a process performed, not logically compressed, but as a full reversal of the process, i.e. such as the process factually occurs.

Based on the dialectical formula, and not the formula of everyday logic. Engels (*Socialism: Utopian and Scientific*) on 'everyday logic'.[15]

Movement based on the trinomial formula is less economical, less rational. But only in the expenditure of movement (of the actor). For it is much more economical in the expenditure of the reader's (viewer's) energy.

This is likewise true for art.

We've not observed two cases of an ability to construct 'readable expressiveness'—form.

Let us venture to extract their *common denominator* and see if it doesn't contain the secret of readable-perceptible form in general.[16]

Non-metaphorical precedes metaphorical.

The full process—the *unverdichtet* [unconsolidated] trinomial A-C-B precedes the consolidated binomial A-B.

We can therefore say that in both cases, in order to receive readable form, our 'subjects' had to be *plastically returned* to one level back down the general ladder of the evolution of thought.

Hence, the question arises: perhaps here is the key to the mystery of form in general?

Let us take a number of examples and see what we do in a work of art.

(1) *Potemkin* and the doctor's pince-nez.

Synecdoche.

Pars pro toto.

Bear's tooth—bear—bear's strength.

Note the *heightened* emotional effect of this in comparison with a presentation of the whole (Gauguin on Turner).[17]

(2) Interesting to compare writers' drafts: 'Taras in the wagon train', 'Es flogen die Gänse' [The geese flew away]. 'There arrived some guests.'

(Note also in both cases the faceless 'Es' and 'there arrived'—neutral—not accidentally *genus neutrum*.)[18]

Citation from Engels (first the movement, and then *what* moves).[19]

'The guests arrived'—'There arrived some guests.'

Heightened poetic quality:

'Die Gänse flogen. Es flogen die Gänse.'

(3) $2 \times 2 \neq 3 + 1$ (Why *funny*, we shall explain another time. For now it is sufficient that it 'gets through' and 'works'.)

Wherein lies the secret of its effectiveness? In the substitution of a numerical abstraction on our level by geometrical representations of an earlier stage of development.

$2 \times 2 \; \boxplus \; 3 + I \; \vdash\!\vdash\!\dashv \; + \; \dashv$

Traces of this can be found wherever you wish.

Especially in Chinese mathematics.

In practice, the Chinese have no objective concept of sizes and distances—they are inseparable from subjective activities of manipulating concrete objects:

(1) the height of a soldier is indicated without considering the head ('soldiers don't need a head', and not in the sense of a *jeu de mots* [play on words], but factually—in terms of his duties, he is 'interesting' only up to his shoulders);

(2) the distance into town is indicated by multiplying by two (for you have to go back);

(3) there exists a concept of *hundred*, but not as *one-hundred units*: in different areas of China, this is 92.87 and even 762 and 56!—i.e. simply *many*.[20]

For them, three is not two plus one, but a member of a different clan, the clan of even and odds: Yin and Yang.[21]

Philosophically, 12345678 is important as an intertwining of two sources.

But tangibly—pure geometry.

Hence, two 'emits' three.

One 'decomposes' into two.

All evens are identical.

All odds are identical.

Similar traces exist in all languages—precisely in other languages, for you recognize this, not when studying a language (when you enter directly into the element of language), but through the mistakes of a foreigner using a language not native to him. [. . .][22]

Mexicans have one general expression for 'many' and 'too many' (*mucho*) and in English, instead of saying 'much', they say 'too mucho', etc.

The heightened reaction—laughter.

(4) From production practice.

The common stage direction: He approaches.

How this happens.

You must have a large selection of personal observations and images of ways of walking. 'The director acts for everyone.'

Today you are—Prince Vasili with a bouncy gait.[23]

Tomorrow you are—Sobakevich, stepping on toes.[24]

The day after tomorrow—flitting Taglioni.[25]

Or three lame men.

Moreover—a certain Richard III in *different acts*. Within the acts, in *different* states. Or Maretskaya in *The Village Schoolteacher* at *different* ages, etc.[26]

And, in order to do this, you must have, instead of a generalized walk that says nothing to the director, an infinite set of particular ways of walking, from which to draw experience for each particular case.

And, finding yourself suddenly on a theatrical stage, you cease being a professor, a doctor, etc., and switch over to the system of thinking of the Klamaths (citation from Lévy-Bruhl).[27]

And every such individual phenomenon of walking gives you (and the viewer) a concretely sensuous sensation of a living, individual image, and not some abstract walking.

Now let us compare the common features in all our examples.

(1) In all four cases we had not only a lowering of the category of thought, but a lowering to an absolutely specific category.

To the category where *pars pro toto* predominates; movement is registered before the object is recognized; abstractly mathematical concepts are not yet separated from concretely geometrical concepts; concepts of particular ways of walking instead of the concept-idea, 'to walk'.

What is this realm?

The realm of sensuous thought, pre-logic, whatever you want to call it!

(2) And in each case we found a heightened *effectiveness of perception* —that is, a heightened *sensuous effect*.

Each time we translated the 'logical thesis' into the language of sensuous speech, of sensuous thought, and as a result we found a heightened *sensuous* effect.

And you can further accept on faith that the whole fund of pre-logical, sensuous thought serves as a fund of the language of form. (I don't like saying 'formal devices'.)

And that there is *not a single phenomenon* of form which could not develop from this fund -could not wholly result from it.

This is a fact.

This is a necessity.

But, as they say in mathematics: 'necessary, but not sufficient.'

Let us take our last example of walking.

Is this reconstruction of the 'Klamath situation' exact and total?

Is the 'reverse submergence' in this stage exact and total?

Yes and no.

For it is not just a submergence.

All of Maretskaia's ways of walking are simultaneously united in the generalization of Maretskaia as an image of a schoolteacher.

However Richard III may walk, he will never start moving like Taglioni, Sobakevich, or Prince Vasili!

Thus, not only a scattering but also a unity.

Or take the example $2 \times 2 \neq 3 + 1$.

Tell this to a person who has not reached the level of abstract numerical concepts—i.e. who does not possess simultaneously a memory (subconscious—not formulative, but *active*) of former stages (memory as *a return* to these stages) and the full, modern stage of development of consciousness—*and we won't get anything*.

And from this we finally derive a formula of what takes place and what is produced by that mysterious 'image' in which, as they say, an artist thinks.

The dialectics of the artistic image.

National in form and socialistic in content.[28]

As such.

As high point of line.

plant—crystal

animal—plant

man—animal

'God'—man.[29]

What we are doing.

Generals cry.

Plunging 'back' to the stage of sensuous thought, we lessen partial control.

We compel the viewer to believe (firing slings at the enemy so Chapayev can swim across), to experience and to cry.[30]

Here a representation is *equal* to a living man.

A flat screen. (cf. the sorcery of sticking pins in wax images of the enemy. A housemaid pokes out the eyes of a photograph of her unfaithful lover.)[31]

Here, a part works for the whole, etc. The history of why in certain moments, certain traits become leading. *Par example. Pars pro toto* and the nineteenth century—a culmination in impressionism—degradation and disintegration into decadence. To where we are plunging them back. To paradise. To the stage of non-differentiating thought. But also the pre-class stage. And therein lies the fascination.

22 November 1947

An excursus on intonation—a sound gesture.

Intonation as the basis of melody.

Gesture as the basis of the plastic arts.

The combination of the two as the basis of audio-visual counterpoint.

The correlation and interconnection within sensuously conscious functioning as the basis of an image.

An image of thought as a unity of the sensuous and the conscious —the prototype of an artistic image.

NOTES

1 The proceedings of the All-Union Creative Conference of Soviet Filmworkers, held in Moscow on 8–13 January 1935 were published under the conference slogan 'Za bol'shoe kinoiskusstvo' [For a Great Cinema Art] later that year. See: Marie Seton, *Sergei M. Eisenstein: A Biography*, REVD EDN (London: Dennis Dobson, 1978), pp. 330–50. E's speeches are translated in: *ESW3*, pp. 16–46.

2 Almost simultaneously with his notes on the psychology of art, E began an article in September 1947, 'Pokhvala kinokhronike' ['In Praise of Film Newsreel'], which was first published in the journal *Kinovedcheskie zapiski* 36–7 (1997–98), pp. 104–14. In it he defines the newsreel as the first stage of the 'artistic' ['khudozhestvennyi', the term used in Russian for 'feature'] film, comparing it with the process of the evolution of graphic art, for which cave-wall drawings and ornaments served as the same sort of first stage. Developing this analogy, E compares the 'single point-of-view' newsreel of the 'Pathé Journal' type (i.e. the simple, automatic recording of a fragment of reality) with the stage of 'outlining' in graphic art, and the 'wise newsreel'

(such as Dziga Vertov's *Cine-Pravda* [Kino-Pravda] and *Cine-Eye* [Kinoglaz]) with the ornament. At the 'ornament stage' such devices as pre-synecdoche (an informational close-up) and pre-montage are invented in the newsreel, which immediately develops into *pars pro toto*, and montage of the third stage, where they then become creative devices of the mature artistic image. The fact that 'Soviet cinema began with the same thing as the first threshold of human culture in general—the chronicle [the Russian word 'khronika' can mean both 'chronicle' and 'newsreel']', was viewed by E as extremely important for the elaboration of methodological principles in the history of cinema. Besides its 'conservational' function (the preservation or recording of a 'past event'), the newsreel was also a unique palliative of 'participation' in a real event—'complicity through reflection and reproduction'. The further natural development of this tendency, immanent to art, E saw in television. Examined here from the viewpoint of the inner logic of the evolution of the screen arts, the tendency of certain post-war films, such as Roberto Rossellini's *Roma, Città aperta* [Italy, 1945], to imitate the style of the newsreel was regarded by E as 'aesthetic mannerism'.

3 E probably had in mind the following passage from: Friedrich Engels, *Dialectics of Nature* (C. P. Dutt ed. and trans.) (New York: International Publishers, 1940), p. 208:

> Until Darwin, what was stressed by his present adherents was precisely the harmonious cooperative working of organic nature, how the plant kingdom supplies animals with

nourishment and oxygen, and animals supply plants with manure, ammonia, and carbonic acid. Hardly was Darwin recognized before these same people saw everywhere nothing but *struggle*. Both views are justified within narrow limits, but both are equally one-sided and prejudiced. The interaction of dead natural bodies includes both harmony and collisions, that of living bodies conscious and unconscious co-operation equally with conscious and unconscious struggle. Hence, even in regard to nature, it is not permissible one-sidedly to inscribe only 'struggle' on one's banners. But it is absolutely childish to desire to sum up the whole manifold wealth of historical evolution and complexity in the meagre and one-sided phrase 'struggle for life'. That says less than nothing.

4 Cf. 'The Dramaturgy of Film Form', *ESW1*, pp. 151–60, *ER*, pp. 93–110; translated as 'A Dialectic Approach to Film Form', *FiFo*, pp. 45–63.

5 The thirtieth anniversary of the 1917 October Revolution was celebrated in November 1947 because of the change in Soviet Russia in February 1918 from the Julian to the Gregorian Calendar.

6 E has in mind here the directorial theories of three of the leading directors in Russian and Soviet theatre in the 20th century: Konstantin S. Stanislavsky (1863–1938), Vsevolod E. Meyerhold (1874–1940) and Alexander Ia. Tairov (1885–1950), one of the founders of Moscow's Kamerny [Chamber] Theatre. In his *Direction* [Rezhissura], written in 1934 (*IP4*, p. 432),

E compares the seemingly irreconcilable methods of Stanislavsky and Meyerhold, seeing in them a dialectical interconnection. The opposition in which the 'internal' and 'constructional' or 'Constructivist' schools stand is not one of 'metaphysics', but of natural stages. Each is a response, in its system and methods, to a certain phase in the evolution of thought —not just artistic thought, but thought in general. In both schools, E perceived 'the mistake of a mechanical *pars pro toto*—an extension of its portion of the cognition of truth to truth as a whole'—whether the 'dictatorship of the irrational (pre-logic)' or the 'dictatorship of the ultra-rational (formal logic).

7 E refers here to the principle of 'totality', one of the basic ideas underlying Meyerhold's theory of 'biomechanics', according to which the whole body participates in any movement. Thus, for example, a movement of the hands starts 'from the feet'. In his 1923 article 'Vyrazitel'noe dvizhenie' ['Expressive Movement'] (see *Millennium Film Journal* 3 [Winter/Spring 1979]) E discusses the findings of many researchers in the field of psychology and physical training (Rudolph Bode, Ludwig Klages, François Delsarte). In a journal entry dated 30 September 1946, he compared his own conception of expressive movement with the 'forty-four principles' of biomechanics (*IP4*, p. 751):

> [O]f all those principles, only one was productive. The first one, the alpha and omega of the theoretical baggage on expressive movement, derived from studies on biomechanics, fits entirely into thesis no. 1 (and no. 16, as a direct derivative of the first):

1.Biomechanics is based wholly on the theory that, if the tip of the nose works, the whole body works. The whole body participates in the working of the most insignificant organ . . .

16. A gesture is the result of the work of the whole body.

And that is all . . . All else in my teaching of expressive movement is MY OWN.

Cf. 'The Montage of Film Attractions', *ESW1*, pp. 39–58; *ER*, pp. 35–52.

8 E deals with this scene in 'Montage 1937', *ESW2*, pp. 16–21. See also: V. Nizhny, *Lessons with Eisenstein* (Ian Montagu and Jay Leyda eds) (London: Allen & Unwin, 1962), pp. 3–18.

9 (E's note) At this point we must not yet say 'sensuous', but 'visual'. 'Non-metaphorical' but not 'pre-metaphorical', which we shall say after analysing a case of refusal.

[Editor's note] I have changed the translation from 'retraction' in the original publication to 'refusal of movement' [otkaznoe dvizhenie], the name derived from Meyerhold's usage in biomechanics and applied by E to what he considered the principle on which stage movement must be constructed. In *Method* he wrote: ' It consists of the fact that, for any motion to be clearly perceived, it must always be preceded by a lesser, preliminary movement in the opposite direction. In such a case, the motion in which we are interested (and which comes second) will not commence imperceptibly, from a "dead halt", but at an abrupt change of contrasting movements. The range of the movement will be the greater. Its visibility, coming second, will be more distinct etc.'

10 E often proposed this example to his students as an illustration of how the staging of movement requires the 'reversal of a metaphorical meaning'. Thus, if the task is to depict a detective 'sticking' to his suspect, the director must visualize this as a concrete action: 'Picture a man following in another's footsteps; when the latter stops, so does the former; he keeps always the same distance' (Nizhny, *Lessons with Eisenstein*, p. 50).

11 Johann Gottfried Gregory (1631–75) was a German pastor who organized the first dramatic performance in Russia. In *Direction*, in a chapter entitled 'On Refusal of Movement', E traces the origin of this principle back to 17th-century Lutheran 'school dramas' (*IP4*, pp. 83–4).

12 Ichikawa Sadanji II (1880–1940) was an outstanding artist of the Japanese Kabuki theatre. E met Sadanji during the Kabuki's visit to Moscow. Hanamichi (literally, 'flower path') is a raised platform running through the auditorium and used as an extension of the stage primarily for the characters' entrances and exits. In *Direction* (*IP4*, p. 84) E wrote that the principle of 'refusal of movement' underlay Sadanji's technique as well: 'Muscovites might recal . . . the performance of the great Sadanji . . . along the hanamichi: three steps forward, a big step back; another three forward and a step—twice as big—back. At greater and greater speed. With greater and greater intensity.'

13 Mei Lan-fan (1894–1961) was a Chinese classical actor famed for his performance of female roles on stage. E met him in Moscow in 1935 and dedicated the

article 'To the Magician of the Pear Orchard' (*ESW3*, pp. 56–67) to him.

14 E has in mind Lenin's definition of the dialectics of cognition: 'The movement of cognition *to* the object can always only proceed dialectically: to retreat in order to hit more surely—*reculer pour mieux sauter* (*savoir?*) [French for: 'to retreat in order better to jump (know?)']: V. I. Lenin, *Philosophical Notebooks* in *Collected Works*, VOL. 38 (Moscow: Foreign Languages Publishing House, 1961), pp. 279–80. E also cites this passage in relation to 'retracted motion' in *Direction* (*IP4*, pp. 84–5).

15 Friedrich Engels, *Anti-Dühring* (C. P. Dutt ed., E. Burns trans.) (New York: International Publishers, 1939), pp. 27–8:

> To the metaphysician, things and their mental images, ideas, are isolated, to be considered one after the other part from each other, rigid, fixed objects of investigation given once for all. He thinks in absolutely discontinuous antitheses. His communication is: 'Yea, yea, Nay, nay, for whatsoever is more than these cometh of evil.' For him a thing either exists, or it does not exist; it is equally impossible for a thing to be itself and at the same time something else. Positive and negative absolutely exclude one another; cause and effect stand in an equally rigid antithesis one to the other. At first sight this mode of thought seems to us extremely plausible, because it is the mode of thought of so-called sound common sense. But sound common sense, respectable fellow as he is

within the homely precincts of his own four walls, has most wonderful adventures as soon as he ventures out into the wide world of scientific research.

16 (E's note) We cannot yet say a 'co-experienceable' and 'experienceable' form-image.

17 See: Paul Gauguin, *The Writings of a Savage* (Daniel Guérin ed.) (New York: Viking, 1978), pp. 145–7.

18 Cf. *ESW3*, pp. 38–9; *FiFo*, pp. 139–40.

19 E has in mind the following passage from Engels' *Socialism: Utopian and Scientific*, cited here from: Karl Marx and Friedrich Engels, *Selected Works in Two Volumes*, VOL. 2 (Moscow: Foreign Languages Publishing House, 1962), p. 129:

> When we consider and reflect upon Nature at large or the history of mankind or our own intellectual activity, at first we see the picture of an endless entanglement of relations and reactions, permutations and combinations, in which nothing remains what, where and as it was, but everything moves, changes, comes into being and passes away. We see, therefore, at first the picture as a whole, with its individual parts still more or less kept in the background; we observe the movements, transitions, connections, rather than the things that move, combine and are connected.

20 E has borrowed his examples from: A. H. Smith, *Chinese Characteristics*, (New York: Fleming H. Revell, 1894), pp. 49–50.

21 In *Method*, E analyses a number of Oriental and Western paintings in terms of this fundamental concept of Chinese philosophy. See: Sergei Eisenstein, *Cinématisme: peinture et cinéma* (A. Zouboff trans.) (Brussels: Editions Complexe, 1980), pp. 157–219.

22 A brief example has been omitted here, describing an incorrect expression untranslatable into English used by Eisenstein's Latvian-born chief cameraman, Eduard K. Tisse, for whom Russian was a second language.

23 Prince Vasili is a character in Tolstoy's *War and Peace*.

24 Sobakevich is a character in Gogol's *Dead Souls*.

25 Marie Taglioni (1804–84) was an Italian ballerina who often performed in Russia.

26 Vera P. Maretskaya (1906–78) was the Soviet actress who played the title role in Mark Donskoi's *Sel'skaia uchitel'nitsa* [The Village Schoolteacher, 1947].

27 E has in mind the following passage in: Lucien Lévy-Bruhl, *How Natives Think* (L.A. Clare trans.) (Princeton, NJ: Princeton University Press, 1985), p. 173: 'The Klamath Indians have no generic term for fox, squirrel, butterfly or frog; but each species has its own name.'

28 In *Method*, E analyses this definition of 'Socialist Realism', seeing in it a dialectical unity of levels of consciousness:

> Here it is quite clearly indicated, first, that form and content relate to different levels of social systems and concepts; second, that these levels are interconnected *by stages* and become separated form each other at a certain phase of development; third, that the unity of form and content is achieved through an

organic unity of both of these levels of consciousness in a work of art. Evolutionally, the
concepts 'national' and 'socialistic' truly stand
precisely in such interrelationships, and the
harmonic unity of both is socially permitted
by the *structure* of Soviet society and state;
aesthetically—in the style of Socialist Realism
—these social principles are reflected in the
realm of literature and art.

29 In *Method*, E analyses the embodiment in art of the
'kingdoms of nature' which separate from each other at
a certain stage of evolution:

In order for a representative of each 'kingdom'
to take shape in a work of art, it must take on
the from of a representative of the 'preceding'
kingdom! In order to enter art, i.e. in order to
find an image, in order to join in form and
style: a plant borrows the structure of a min-
eral; an animal—of a plant; a human—of an
animal; a divinity—the form of a human!

30 A reference to the final scene of the Vasilievs' film
Chapayev [1934] as one example of the phenomenon
by which audiences accept events depicted on the
screen as reality. During screenings of *Chapayev* boys
in the audience are reputed to have fired slingshots at
the enemy: *IP2*, p. 114n.

31 These examples are discussed in greater detail in:
ESW3, pp. 37–8; *FiFo*, pp. 142–4.

THE PSYCHOLOGY OF
COMPOSITION[1]

In an issue of *L'Esprit nouveau* for 1921, Juan Gris wrote:

> I work with the elements of this intellect, with the
> imagination. I try to make concrete that which is
> abstract. I proceed from the general to the partic-
> ular, by which I mean that I start with an
> abstraction in order to arrive at a true fact.
>
> I want to endow the elements I use with a
> new quality; starting from general types I want to
> construct particular individuals.
>
> I consider that the architectural element in
> painting is mathematics, the abstract side;[2] I want
> to humanize it. Cézanne turns a bottle into a
> cylinder, but I begin with a cylinder and create an

individual of a special type: I make a bottle—a particular bottle—out of a cylinder. Cézanne tends towards architecture, I tend away from it. That is why I compose with abstractions (colours) and make my adjustments when these colours have assumed the form of objects. For example, I make a composition with a white and a black and make adjustments when the white has become a paper and the black a shadow: what I mean is that I adjust the white so that is becomes a paper and the black so that it becomes a shadow.

This painting is to the other what poetry is to prose.[3]

••

Along with Juan Gris, let us cite another pronouncement.

From a different epoch.

From a different time.

And even from—a different realm of craftsmanship.

All the more clear will be the picture of the common working method of artists—whether they deal with the spectrum of colours, the scale of sounds, or words and verbal images.

Our example concerns a man from a different century —the nineteenth.

From a different continent—he is an American.

And not a painter, but a poet.

We shall dwell on a work of his in which he described his own process of work on his best known creation.

This is Edgar Allan Poe's article, 'The Philosophy of Composition', which describes how he wrote The Raven.[4]

This work is, on the whole, very well known, and I shall therefore limit myself to those excerpts which relate directly to the process by which colour images arise, which we outlined and traced through the works of the Spanish painter mentioned above.[5]

To this day, this article has continued to remain an object of controversy among the most diverse authors.

Hanns Heinz Ewers, a not very successful imitator of Poe in many ways, enthusiastically extols this work as the first model of a detailed picture of 'the logic of artistic creation'.[6]

The majority of critics refuse to take this work at face value.

And many even consider it the same sort of typical 'hoax' in the field of literary criticism, such as Poe had perpetrated in the field of journalism by means of the notorious sensation he caused in the newspaper, the *New York Sun* ('The Transatlantic Flying Machine of Mr. Monck Mason'), concerning the flight of a hot-air balloon, the 'Victoria', which not only had never flown anywhere, but which had never even existed.

All this was later published in the form of a story, 'The Balloon-Hoax', with an explanatory preface by the author. But at the time of its publication in the newspaper, this diary of the flight created an unimaginable sensation 'during the few hours'—as Poe writes—'intervening between a couple of the Charleston mails'.

'And, in fact, if (as some assert)'—Poe further adds with almost Twainian logic—'the "Victoria" did not absolutely accomplish the voyage recorded, it will be difficult to assign a reason why she should not have accomplished it.'[7]

The critic, Joseph Wood Krutch, who once visited Moscow long, long ago, considers the whole article simple fabrication, maintaining that 'there is no writer who ever lived who seems less likely than Poe to have created in this way . . .'[8]

But Marie Bonaparte[9] believes that this article and the literary type first invented by Poe—the analytical detective, and even the very genre of the detective novel—as well as individual analytical works such as the truly quite pedantic exposure of 'Maelzel's Chess-Player' or the studies on cryptography ['A Few Words on Secret Writing'] etc.— were intended by the psychologically unbalanced author to convince others—above all himself—that madness was not gradually taking hold of him, that the fantasy which permeates his work is created by him voluntarily, deliberately, fully consciously, 'with the precision and rigid consequence of a mathematical problem' (Poe), totally apart from any irrational impulses and even outside ordinary normal intuition.

I personally believe that the secret of all this controversy lies in the fact that this 'article' on 'the philosophy of composition' is simultaneously and in its own way—a tale. And a tale in that American sense of the word which connotes both a made-up story and literature in one and the same word—fiction.

A tale typical for Poe—a tale belonging, however, not to the group of literary 'hoaxes' such as 'The Balloon-Hoax', but a tale belonging to the group of detective stories.

And constructed entirely in the manner of the model most typical for his whole genre—'The Purloined Letter'— with the sole difference that here the partially revealed letter also remains partially concealed to the very end.

For in the present case, Poe is not quite willing to solve the mystery and bring it out into the clear, bright light of day.

And to this end, he intentionally sends the reader along a trail of cunningly conceived wrong conclusions about the main thing ('red herrings')—a trail of deliberately placed, misleading, incidental clues.

It is usually said that the technique of the detective novel requires that, as soon as the precise motive has been established, the identity of the criminal must be revealed[10]—and the whole mystery solved overall.

We shall proceed in exactly the same way.

We shall attempt to discover the true motive behind the writing of this article.

And then, it will become clear that the very form of an investigation serves here merely as a compositional modification of an endlessly repeated theme—so as not to be boring, as Poe himself writes in this very article about the incessant modification (for the same purpose) of the compositional elaboration of the unvaried refrain, 'Nevermore'.

And from this viewpoint, we shall see that the true incentive, the true motive for writing this analysis of 'The Raven', will prove to be not so much the essence of the analysis, as the very same thing which in reality induced the author to write 'The Raven' itself in the first place.

(And specifically about this, Poe remains silent in the article:

Let us dismiss, as irrelevant to the poem per se, the circumstance—or say, the necessity—which, in the first place, gave rise to the intention of composing a poem that should suit at once the popular and the critical taste.)[11]

And this motive, in my opinion, turns out to be the very same that brought to life not only 'The Raven', but also Annabel Lee, 'Morella', 'Ligeia', 'Bernice' and Lenore, if we restrict ourselves to the most basic embodiments of this stimulating motive.

However let us pause here.

We ourselves shall introduce here a moment of 'in-hibition', obligatory for the detective novel, preceding the solution.

For our basic interest lies in the phases and aspects of the creative process.

Starting from the very beginning with the misleading title, 'The Philosophy of Composition', Poe chose not to use for this detective story of his *couleur locale* in the form of some mediaeval castle in ruins, the terrifying hideouts of city riff-raff, the laboratories of secret experiments where Frankensteins are fabricated, or the wretched, hermetically sealed room on the rue Morgue, into which a gorilla with a razor sneaks through a chimney.

Here, the role of the clues to be read and solved by the detective is played by the changing phases of the creative process, and the individual nooks and crannies of its labyrinth, which are successively penetrated by the brilliant, blinding rays of logic, serve as the objects of the mysteries to be unravelled.

And here—in keeping with the strictest observance of the genre's laws—another condition of the detective novel or story is fulfilled (and also, incidentally, of fantastic literature, where again our author is a shining example).

This is the absolute authenticity of the individual, concrete elements of the narrative.

(Only under this condition is genuine fantastic quality acquired by that which is driven beyond the limits of credibility of logical appearance in the realm of the incredible.)

Poe adheres throughout to this sort of conscientious and truthful setting forth of the very elements of the process.

But let us briefly recount the analysis itself and those features of it which truthfully and accurately outline the phases of the creative process in which we are interested.

And let us save for the end our concise detective review of the evidence exposing the true motives of the work itself, as is required by another fine tradition of the detective novel: only after the climax—the apogee of the very act of unmasking the criminal—do you concisely and lucidly go over the links which formed the chain of the final unravelling.

The initial consideration was that of extent. If any literary work is too long to be read at one sitting, we must be content to dispense with the immensely important effect derivable from unity of impression—for, if two sittings be required, the affairs of the world interfere, and everything like totality is at once destroyed . . .

Holding in view these considerations, as well as that degree of excitement which I deemed not above the popular, while not below the critical, taste, I reached at once what I conceived the proper length for my intended poem—a length of about one hundred lines. It is, in fact, a hundred and eight.

My next thought concerned the choice of an impression, or effect, to be conveyed: and here I may as well observe that, throughout the construction, I kept steadily in view the design of rendering the work universally appreciable . . . that pleasure which is at once the most intense, the most elevating, and the most pure, is, I believe, found in the contemplation of the beautiful. When, indeed, men speak of Beauty, they mean, precisely, not a quality, as is supposed, but an effect—they refer, in short, just to that intense and pure elevation of soul—not of intellect, or of heart—upon which I have commented, and which is experienced in consequence of contemplating 'the beautiful'...

Regarding, then, Beauty as my province, my next question referred to the tone of its highest manifestation —and all experience has shown that this tone is one of sadness. Beauty of whatever kind, in its supreme development, invariably excites the sensitive soul to tears. Melancholy is thus the most legitimate of all the poetical tones.

The length, the province, and the tone, being thus determined, I betook myself to ordinary induction, with the view of obtaining some artistic piquancy which might serve me as a key-note in the construction of the poem—some pivot upon which the whole structure might turn. In carefully thinking over all the usual artistic effects—or more properly points, in the theatrical sense—I did not fail to perceive immediately that no one had been so universally employed as that of the refrain ... I resolved to diversify, and so vastly heighten, the effect, by adhering, in general, to the monotone of sound, while I continually varied that of thought: that is to say, I determined to produce continuously novel effects, by the variation of the application of the refrain—the refrain itself remaining, for the most part, unvaried.[12]

Let him believe all he wants that these forms are a true description of the initial phases of the creative process (even though we know that they occur not at the stage of the first impulse, but at the stage of selection)—all the same, taken on their own and individually, each of them is outlined correctly.

At certain moments of creation, all these elements do indeed exist as such.

And the fact that Poe assembles these individual stones into his own arbitrarily organized, preconceived, logical architectonics of the overall process is, perhaps, above all a tribute to Beauty, and not to Truth—in Poe's own precise understanding of these words. And consequently, the essay itself, in keeping with 'the laws established by the poet himself', is, in this sense, not so much an analytical document as . . . a poem. Perhaps unexpected and unusual in form. But a poem.

But this poem, again in keeping with the same conceptions, is a means of avoiding the 'homeliness' of an inevitably attendant passion.

And, therefore, the very fact that we have before us, in the guise of an analytical work, a poem about the composition of The Raven, testifies to the presence here of a flight typical for the author himself: the same escape from the homely prose of real passion to the realm of poetic beauty, which translates real suffering and passion into abstractly musical sound and feeling.

And this already quite clearly tells us that the same and just as clearly tortuous passion underlies this work, as it does the other poems, with the sole difference that this time the author does not want to name it, wants to hide from it and achieves this by hiding it from himself, hiding it from the reader by the tale's unusual form and leading this reader on the wrong trail by even the very title of the article, calling 'philosophy of composition' that which should be called a 'poem', and not at all about 'composition' that which should be called a 'poem', and not at all about 'composition' (and then forcing the analysis to perform on the phases of creation that which the detective does with an interpretation of evidence).

The true content,

the true 'motive' in writing this work will be—in my opinion—not even a self-assurance of one's total and conscious creative freedom (which of all previous interpretations seems the most psychologically persuasive and probably corresponds to the chief—second in intensity—attendant, and not basic, motive).

This motive is, of course, something else.

And this motive, I believe, consists in being able once more, for a second time, through the very same circle of ideas and images in 'The Raven'—and, perhaps, for the tenth time in general—to experience the same sweet agony of the basic theme of love for a dead or dying young girl, who stands as a personal lyrical tragedy over both the real-life biography of the author, and hence over his entire creative work.

This poetically animated, central image of Edgar Allan Poe's works is touchingly concrete, and that is probably the reason why,—in contrast to another poet's obsessive image of a 'beautiful lady'—though embodied a countless number of times, it bears an endless diversity of strange-sounding, but concrete names, and is never simply called . . . 'The Stranger'.[13]

Its distant prototype vaguely recalls Poe's young mother—the actress Elizabeth Arnold, who died of consumption when the poet was two-and-a-half years old. And the real 'model' was Poe's own young wife, who died just as tragically from the same disease—his cousin, Virginia Clemm.

This wedding had been a secret one in view of the fact of her parents' opposition to it.

Because of the bride's age.

She was just barely thirteen.

Precisely thus, as a prototype of Lenore, is Virginia described in the diary of one of Poe's later friends of many

years—one of the 'starry sisterhood', Elizabeth Oakes
Smith:

> The first time I ever saw Mr Poe, he called upon
> me with his pretty child-wife, who must have been
> to him as near as anything earthly could be,
> 'Lenore', with her long lustrous eyes, and serious
> lovely face.[14]

But the Reverend George Gilfillan accuses Poe of
having hastened the death of his wife so that he could
write The Raven. Poe's clashes with 'reverends' were fre-
quent and bitter, even though courteousness and truth
were completely on the side of the poet (see the note to
'The Raven' in the single-volume *The Best Known Works of
Edgar Allan Poe*).[15]

But images of love and death had already merged as
one for Poe in the period between these two dramas, in a
no less tragic episode, at the very moment when his
feelings first began to stir.

From the age of fourteen dates his ardent and
romantic captivation with the mother of one of his school-
mates—Robert Stanard.

But this does not last very long—Jane Stith Stanard
would soon die.

The impression on Poe was terrible (her death was preceded by a mental illness).

According to unconfirmed data, he would wander nightly through the deserted cemetery around her grave.

But it is widely accepted that one of his last, most heartrending poems—To Helen—is dedicated precisely to her.[16]

In either event, the theme of a connection between love and death, the theme of love for a dying, beautiful young woman, becomes a theme inseparable from Poe.

And from this point of view, it seems to me that following 'The Raven' with a pretended analysis of how the poem is put together, is above all, a second, repeated experiencing of the very same circle of images and ideas, clothed in the same images and forms, with which the Raven itself sang the author's favourite theme.

In essence—a direct refrain.

But a 'refrain' clothed in such an unexpected, original form, that many, many generations have failed to solve it, thrown off the trail by the system of 'false clues' cunningly placed by the author.

Poe's persistent inclination towards repetition (not to mention that the device of repetition is one of the basic means of 'The Raven' itself) is noted by even the least inspired, perhaps, of all his biographers—Una

Pope-Hennessy, who points out the intensification of this otherwise normal tendency under the influence of Poe's weakness for narcotics:

> We all develop an automatism to deal with the repetitive acts of life, but Poe seems, by virtue of drugs, to have carried over into the world of imagination an automatism of his own which resulted in a perpetual thrumming on the same string.[17]

This analysis of 'The Raven', following 'The Raven' itself, strikes me as a manifestation of this same tendency towards repetition.[18]

Simply repeat oneself?

Simply write a variation on the same theme, in the same rhythms or in the same images?

For an unreserved champion of originality above all—this would be inconceivable and impossible.

He writes with regard to himself that the choice, not only of the means, not only of the theme, but of even the very future effect of the work is made by him, '... keeping originality always in view—for he is false to himself who ventures to dispense with so obvious and so easily attainable a source of interest.'[19]

And then to satisfy the need to go once again through the experiences dear to him in 'The Raven', he actually does choose a form that is the most 'original'.

He chooses the only form that truly enables him to creatively retrace his own work, its individual parts, its peculiarities, its stages of coming into being, and, at the same time, to do this in the apparent guise of something quite different and quite new—he chooses the form of an analysis and history of the creation of his own work.

But moreover—this second experience affords him the possibility of dissecting his beloved images, as in an anatomical theatre, finding in this a special voluptuousness that is gripping for him and those in whom the concepts of love and death are bound as one, for those in whom a living face and a decaying face of death are capable of evoking an identical lyrical shudder.

Are we not familiar with the stories about Dante Gabriel Rossetti, who for many years hid the coffin of his dead wife and mournfully revelled in the sight of the preserved cascades of her golden blonde hair.[20]

And Poe, of course, in defiance of this direct, primitive, 'straight' path, chooses a much more refined, 'original' way of satisfying this need—not by concealing the real crypt, but by dissecting the swarm of images dear to him, in which the theme dear to him is expressed—by means of a quite poetically conceived analysis of the creative process, actually conducted above all so as to 'dissect like a corpse' the music of his beloved images with the scalpel of analysis.[21]

'Never before him did any one so dismember his own work of art, and dissect it to its last shred ...', writes Hanns Heinz Ewers.[22]

'Dismembered' [zergliedert], 'to its last shred' [letzte Faser], 'dissected' [zersetzt]—these very terms from the field of physiological dissection, in which the process of Poe's 'literary analysis' presents itself to the detached observer, already testify to how sharply there is felt here— under the guise of a seemingly coldly logical, mathematical analysis of literary form—the genuine, terrifying process of cutting into pieces the living image, brought to life by the poet himself.

Cutting into it, the poet himself experiences the same strange and unique, alien and incomprehensible feeling of voluptuous 'delight in self-torture' that he attributes to his own hero, forcing him to compound his grief by posing questions to which he already awaits the well-known answer, 'Nevermore', and among them the one he fears the most: will he see his Lenore in other worlds?

'Quoth the Raven—Nevermore.'

It seems to me that such a portrait of a substitute—an imagistic replacement of the direct motive by an allegory— is obvious here.

But it would be possible to cite yet another example from the practice of the self-same Poe, this time shrouding the actual act of decomposition[23] again in the form of an analysis.

With the sole difference that here Poe performs his analytical autopsy in the form of a literary analysis on an image created by himself, whereas in the other case—by means of analytical deductions of a detective-like nature, concerning the murder of a girl entirely unknown to him—Marie Rogêt, the details of which were supposedly taken from newspaper articles.

At the base of this story lies the actual, unsolved murder of a certain Mary Rogers in New York, to which Poe devoted keen attention.

This is entirely understandable, for this activity, too, had entered the circle of the most—by his own admission—'poetic subjects on a melancholic theme', and in its material somewhere inside called to mind one of his most precious recurring leitmotifs, defining his own melancholy.

Quite interesting and fully in support of my comparison is the brief description (very brief—in two lines, and therefore undoubtedly the more gripping in relief!)

given 'The Mystery of Marie Rogêt', again by Pope-Hennessy: 'Police reports and a study in the decomposition of the human body play a great part in the narrative.'[24]

It is interesting that Pope-Hennessy writes not even 'disintegration', but 'decomposition', which equally corresponds to the concept of the decay and breaking down of the body after death.

And this already fully establishes the kinship of both works and the unity of motive in theme: for the analysis of 'The Raven' is exactly this kind of obsessive 'de-composition' by means of an examination of the magnificent image of 'perfect Beauty', created by him in his poem.

In comparing 'The Mystery of Marie Rogêt' with the analysis of 'The Raven', we see that both cases have to do with 'substitutes', the different appearances taken on by the refrain-like persistence of the poet's theme.

In this sense, the very refrain-like structure of 'The Raven' is also, first and foremost, an 'autobiographical projection'—this time on to the structure of the work, and not a result of cold calculation.

And the difference between the two lies only in the degree to which the initial image which moved Poe is transformed, as unarrangeable investigations of the 'decomposition' of a lifeless body turn into de-composition 'for the purposes of analysis' of the body of the poem.

And at the very lowest extreme of such a graded ranking of 'substitutes' might stand—and may the memory of the great poet, however ironic and sarcastic, forgive me and not take offence beyond the grave!—that curious company which I happened to stumble across in pre-Nazi Berlin.[25]

The company was in the business of supplying the suffering, on the basis of a photograph, with as precise as possible a substitute of the girl he hopelessly dreamt of . . . One man was captivated by the unattainable Greta Garbo or Marlene Dietrich. Another—by a childhood sweetheart who had married someone else. A third—like Edgar Allan Poe—by a long dead object of adoration. The means of substitution were the most diverse. And the company did splendid business.

We have kept our attention focused on this question of a substitute.

We have examined it not only in the form in which Lenore herself, as a poetic, generalized image of the majority of his heroines, replaces the merged together, forever lost and eternally mourned Elizabeth Arnold, Jane Stanard and Frances Allan.[26]

We have also traced it at the stage of almost total dematerialization in the form of a seemingly completely abstracted analysis.

From there, we descended to the almost clinically straightforward solution of the same thing in the form of a police story about 'The Mystery of Marie Rogêt'.

We were not even too squeamish to recall the hardly attractive factory of actual substitutes, organized by the practical Berliners, the worthy kin of those who later established huge salvage enterprises utilizing the human skin, human fat and hair which issued forth from Fascist concentration camps.

We have not lingered upon this theme of a substitute in vain. In later chapters, while discussing the theme of the scenario on Pushkin and shading it in with features from the biography of Chaplin, we shall deal with this question in a different dramatic context.[27] So let this slightly detailed reference to this theme serve as a first introduction to one of the leitmotifs of future chapters.

Now that we know the true motive and the true emotional purpose underlying the poem itself, we can define more precisely, step by step, and reread everything that Poe writes.

In view of this, the material of the article is naturally divided into three categories.

We can dismiss as false all declarations and arguments to the effect that the poem was written without any ulterior motive or necessity—solely as a 'calculation of effect' (Poe's own emphasis—that it was the author's design 'to render it manifest that no one point in its composition is referable either to accident or intuition—that the work proceeded, step by step, to its completion with the precision and rigid consequence of a mathematical problem'.[28]

We shall also refuse to take into consideration the author's condescending and haughty claim: 'Let us dismiss, as irrelevant to the poem per se, the circumstance—or, say, the necessity—which, in the first place, gave rise to the intention of composing a poem that should suit at once the popular and the critical taste.'[29]

We fully agree with the author that such a necessity, of course, will help very little in understanding the poem, but we also know that the basic necessity in writing not only the poem, but even this post-factum analysis of its composition, arises from an entirely different and clearly genuine necessity of the author, putting it crudely, to long for Lenore, to 'torture himself' with her memory.

And it is to this necessity, to this stimulus, to this driving motive, that we shall turn our attention, first and foremost, as the true source of all those peculiarities, which Poe himself would like to portray as homunculi of pure abstraction engendered in laboratory retorts.

The second group of the article's material is made up of all kinds of ideas of a generally constructive and compositional nature, having no strictly direct relation to the embodiment of that theme which, despite the author's claims, did not at all get its attractiveness, profundity, and tragic emotionality from mathematical abstractions.

This also relates to the article's first sentence, paradoxical at first glance, but unfortunately, all too rarely applicable in practice, to the effect that a work should be written from end to beginning. That one should know precisely in what direction, at what point and in what way the point of apogee occurs, or where the peripeteia should lead the hero, before starting to work them out, which is not possible without being precisely orientated towards the final destinations.

This claim, in the categorical form in which Poe states it, is, of course, disputable in many regards.

A calculation here is undoubtedly necessary, but the creative process itself is, of course, much more complex:

it is, above all, a living process—this definition, of course, does not fit within the parameters of the mathematical image that Poe wants to give it.

And as something living—it is subject to change and growth in the very process of its development.

Here, I do not at all mean what Picasso says about the creative process—as a process truly without any sense of purpose.

Rather, I should like to cite an example such as the novel, 'War and Peace', which, as is well known, from the stage of initial conception to final completion, underwent the most complex regeneration of not only material and treatment, but also the idea, world-outlook and views on history and the role of the individual on the part of Tolstoy himself.

It is interesting that Poe considers these elemental transformations and spawnings in the creative process as something shameful—and especially when the true purpose turns out to have been seized at the last moment, which so crazily corresponds to the truth whenever you are dealing with a broad, emotionally perceived conception, and not with a play à thèse, employed in order 'to enliven the paragraphs'.

He even believes that the 'homeliness' of such elements within the creative process is one of the reasons why the natural modesty of authors causes them to be embarrassed and to refrain from describing the history of the creation of their works.

And Poe allows himself this only to the extent to which he considers himself—or rather, presents himself—

in the pose of being free of all this, and, consequently, a logical creator.

The quite sensible ideas on the extent and length of the poem can be included in this same category.

(Ideas which, incidentally, are quite useful for film-makers, all of whom till now have passed on this problem.)

Such are the discourses on Beauty, Truth, and Passion which we touched on earlier in a different regard, and also the elevating role of poetic beauty as a means of eliciting a universal response to the poem.

And only after this do we come to those elements proper which interest us as a poetic and consequential materialization in concrete images of embodiment of those generalized emotions which serve as the poet's initial stimulus.

The basic emotion which characterizes the poem is sadness.

Its appearance as the basic tonality of the poem, Poe once again justifies by means of a speculatively biased calculation.

> Regarding, then Beauty as my province, my next question referred to the tone of its highest mani-festation—and all experience has shown that this tone is one of sadness. Beauty of whatever kind,

in its supreme development, invariably excites the sensitive soul to tears. Melancholy is thus the most legitimate of all the poetical tones.[30]

Poe assures us that he mathematically 'deduced' melancholy from all the preceding conditions: the necessity of Beauty; sadness as the most supreme manifestation of Beauty; melancholy as the most legitimate embodiment of the tone of sadness.

One page later, he continues this line of reasoning, and through the device of direct questions and answers, he will make his next deduction.

True, in order to once again mislead the reader from the genuine motives behind the writing of the poem, he will preface this with a picture of how this prerequisite gave rise to the principle of the refrain, the sound of the refrain, the refrain itself and thus the image of the raven itself (about which later).

But this passage is clearly inserted into the direct sequence for the obvious purpose of distracting attention from the quite clear contrivance of the line of reasoning.

And, even after this, before he asks himself the final questions, Poe hastily sticks in one more reference to yet another quite untrue 'motive':

Now, never losing sight of the object supremeness, or perfection, at all points, I asked myself—'Of all melancholy topics, what, according to the universal understanding of mankind, is the most melancholy?' Death—was the obvious reply. 'And when,' I said, 'is this most melancholy of topics most poetical?' From what I have already explained at some length, the answer, here also, is obvious—'When it most closely allies itself to Beauty: the death, then, of a beautiful woman is, unquestionably, the most poetical topic in the world—and equally is it beyond doubt that the lips best suited for such a topic are those of a bereaved lover.'[31]

The above-cited line is logically continued:

Melancholy is the most legitimate expression of the tone of sadness; the most melancholy subject is death: the most poetic death is death connected with beauty—ergo, taking into consideration the requirement of unsurpassed perfection above all—the only subject possible is the death of a beautiful young woman, and this can be spoken about most fully only by the lips of one who has lost her.

All mathematically splendid, as splendid as the mathematical deductions of Descartes, Leibniz or Newton.

With just one 'but'.

With the 'but' that here, the process is arranged from foot to head.

And in full accordance with the initial thesis, it is presented here in reverse order—from end to beginning.

At the initial phase stands Poe, himself abandoned, and the dead Lenore who abandoned him (Virginia, who was dying at the time, covered with recollections of Mrs Stanard and Elizabeth Arnold).

An ocean of sadness, flooding the poet's heart with melancholy at the sight of a dying young woman, spreads into the tonal element of sadness.

This, of course, is the real path that the poet überbaut [reconstructs], as though embarrassed for his own personal theme to be displayed in such naked form in the poem.

He needed to substitute the true picture of his direct self-expression with a complex graph of a supposedly mathematical calculation, exactly as he had substituted the true motive in writing yet another work about Lenore— with the form of a supposed analysis of the first.

It was important for us to bring into the picture, by means such as those described by Poe, the true sequence of the origin and appearance of the element of sadness, whose tone truly was clearly transposed (as the second phase of the process) into the structure of the refrain, its rhythm, its verbal image, and the form of its vehicle.

The description of this stage is, for us, perhaps the most interesting one:

> Having made up my mind to a refrain, the division of the poem into stanzas was, of course, a corollary: the refrain forming the close to each stanza. That such a close, to have force, must be sonorous and susceptible of protracted emphasis, admitted no doubt: and these considerations inevitably led me to the long *o* as the most sonorous vowel, in connection with *r* as the most producible consonant.
>
> The sound of the refrain being thus determined, it became necessary to select a work embodying this sound, and at the same time in the fullest possible keeping with that melancholy which I had predetermined as the tone of the poem. In such a search it would have been absolutely impossible to overlook the word 'Nevermore'. In fact, it was the very first which presented itself . . .
>
> I had now gone so far as the conception of a Raven—the bird of ill omen—monotonously repeating the one word, 'Nevermore', at the conclusion of each stanza . . .

I had now to combine the two ideas, of a lover lamenting his deceased mistress and a Raven continuously repeating the word 'Nevermore'.[32]

The choice of 'nevermore' arose from the 'demand' of o and r.

The choice itself of o and r came, of course, not from the motives which he cites, but from their belonging to the name, Lenore and the 'Nevermore' that immediately arose is, of course, above all, a direct rhyme with this still unuttered name.

It is no accident that Poe himself writes: 'In fact, it was the very first which presented itself!'

But . . . all the worse!

As it turns out, this name had been uttered. And not simply so. By Poe himself, in the very same rhyme, and even several years before the writing of 'The Raven' itself. The foregoing idea actually came to me almost instantaneously as I read the motivation of the appearance of o and r. I then decided to take a look at the poem itself which is connected with the name, Lenore. (It appeared under the title, Lenore, in 1843, two years before 'The Raven', which was written in 1844 and published in 1845.[33] 'The Philosophy of Composition' appeared in print in April 1846: the very proximity of dates is already significant.)

And so?

There we find in black and white the following verse:

And, Guy De Vere, hast *thou* no tear?
—weep now or never more!
See! on yon drear and rigid bier low
lies thy love, Lenore![34]

So not only an image of a young, dying girl—an image which constantly haunted Edgar Allan Poe.

Not only this image is linked with the name 'Lenore'.

But also the image which had already crystallized into the rhyme, 'never more—Lenore' (two years later: 'Lenore —Nevermore').

This fact, in my opinion, completely unmasks Edgar Allan Poe. And not so much the fact itself, as his silence about it—about such a thing—about such a significant circumstance in the pages of an analytical work, begun almost polemically, almost with a challenge and so condescendingly—with a question as to why such a paper, before Poe's, 'has never been given to the world'.[35]

There is even a violation here of what is considered a requisite condition in the detective game between the reader and detective-story writer—fair play.

The author has no right to conceal any evidence or information, upon which basis the reader himself would be able to solve the mystery at a certain moment of the novel's development.[36]

He may report them as camouflaged as he likes, as much in passing as he likes, as veiled and in whatever misleading context he likes, but to remain silent, he has no right.

In the present case, Poe concealed evidence, and the most important piece at that, not only for revealing the true motive, but for even a conscientious and thorough account of all the data and circumstances, connected with the trials and solutions of work on 'The Raven'.

Truly, how could he not mention this older and earlier (by two years) worked out assonance between a name and a word, turned so fully not into just an incidental within the poem, but into the most essential thing: through the name of Lenore into the theme, and through the refrain-like 'Nevermore' into the foundation of its form. For the stanza where 'Lenore' and 'Nevermore' meet, Poe himself defines as the climax.

It is the first thing he writes ('. . . it was here, at this point of my preconsiderations, that I first put pen to paper . . .')[37] And even with the conscious aim of making it the most powerful:

'Had I been able, in the subsequent composition, to construct more vigorous stanzas, I should, without scruple, have purposely enfeebled them, so as not to interfere with the climacteric effect.'[38]

Among other 'concealments' from the true process of the creation of 'The Raven', one could also note the fact that before crediting himself with the principle of internal rhymes—the fundamental feature of the poem's structure—Poe had already admired it in the works of another author.

He had run across it in a poem by Elizabeth Barrett Browning ('Lady Geraldine's Courtship').[39]

Moreover, there is even a direct borrowing in 'The Raven'.

Thus Poe's line:

> And the silken, sad, uncertain rustling
> of each purple curtain . . .

borrows not only the principle, rhythm and tone, but even the very rhymes from Miss Barrett's lines:

> With a murmurous stir uncertain in the air
> the purple curtain . . .

Our attention has been drawn to this by Louis Untermeyer, an editor and commentator of an edition of Poe's poems, who considers the dedication by Poe to Miss

Barrett of his collection of verses, *The Raven and Other Poems*, to be something of a poetic tribute or even a kind of compensation.[40]

I think that this circumstance is a terrible blow to the very foundation of the investigatively prejudiced and erroneous, but poetically fully harmonically erected structure of analysis, which must be placed in quotation marks.

For this analysis (taken as a whole), as we see, is nothing more than a rearrangement of the folds in the poet's mourning clothes as he grieves over his lost love, conventionally named Lenore (just as Blok named his recurring vision, 'The Stranger')—mourning and folds, which, in a different combination, formed the tale of 'Morella', the stanzas of 'The Raven' itself, or the suppressed sobbing of Annabel Lee. 'The Philosophy of Composition' is yet one more form, one more aspect, one more recombination of the refrain-like monotony of the obsessive theme of a dead love.

A lament over her, realized 'for variety' (as Poe would say) as an analytical dissection of the body of the poem about a woman, whom death has doomed to decomposition and decay.

Necrophilia!

An anatomical dissection of a living image dedicated to her, possessing a unique—and, of course, cold—

voluptuousness. The coldness of this strange passion is hidden behind the logical 'mathematicalness' of a description of the features of the process, re-emphasized—which cancels itself out—to the extent of a reassurance 'that no one point of its composition is referable either to accident or intuition'.

But at the same time, through its individual components—I would say all of them (especially if they are considered not only within the framework of this one poem)—the process is outlined here precisely.

And if not, perhaps, with an accurate graph of its true development, then, in any case, with an accurate representation of the process in its refined, 'prepared' form—the form in which algebra writes the generalized outcome of x, y, and z in the peripeteia of the solution of equations, without taking into account that in particular embodiments (in geese, apples, bushels of wheat, or tons of coal), in any particular case of a particular outcome, in practice they can also bypass, accidentally omit or solve the problem in their own way, and not coincide fully with the outline of the abstracted contour, which has generalized hundreds of actual particular cases of development of the process into its kind of ideal, 'concentrated' form.

And to complete and crown our series of examples, let us add a missing link through a new pronouncement—consciously programmatic account (through a no less complicated meander) of the creative process of another poet.

This link is full of conscious purpose.

And the full picture behind this is drawn out for us by the pronouncements of Mayakovsky.

My most effective piece of recent verse is, I think, To Sergei Esenin . . . [41]

Esenin's end saddened us with the sadness common to all humanity. But this end immediately appeared completely natural and logical. I heard about it in the night, and my sadness would have probably remained sadness and abated towards morning, had not the morning papers carried his last lines:

In this life there's nothing new in dying, But in living there is nothing newer

After these lines Esenin's death became a fact of literature.[42]

It immediately became clear how many unstable people this powerful poem, precisely a poem, verse, would bring to the noose and the revolver.

And no newspaper analyses or articles could ever erase this poem.

One can and should counter this poem with a poem, and nothing but a poem, verse.

Thus the poets of the USSR were given a social command to write verse about Esenin. An exceptional command, important and urgent, because Esenin's lines began to take effect quickly and unerringly. Many accepted the command. But write what? How?

Having examined his death from all points of view and delved into other people's material, I formulated and set myself the problem.

Pragmatic orientation: deliberately to neutralize the effect of Esenin's last poem, to make his end uninteresting, to replace the bland beauty of death with another kind of beauty—because working humanity needs all its strength for the Revolution which has started, and because in spite of the hardship of the road and the painful contradictions of the NEP, it demands that we glorify the joy of life, the happiness of the immensely difficult march to Communism.

Now that I have the poem in front of me, these things are easy to formulate, but how hard it was when I started writing . . .

I walk about, gesticulating, mumbling still almost without words, now shortening my steps in order not to impede my mumbling, now mumbling more quickly in time to my steps.

Thus is the rhythm hewn and shaped—the rhythm which is the basis of all poetic work and which goes through it like a rumble. Gradually, from this rumbling, one begins to squeeze out single words . . .

First and most frequently, the main word becomes apparent—the main word which characterizes the meaning of the verse or the word which is to be rhymed. The remaining words come and arrange themselves in relation to the main one.

One of the important features of a poem, particularly a tendentious, declamatory one, is the ending. The most successful lines of the poem are usually put in the ending. Sometimes one has to recast the whole verse to justify such an arrangement.

In my poem about Esenin this ending naturally consisted of a rephrasing of Esenin's last lines.

They sound like this:

Esenin's: In this life there's nothing new in dying.
           But to go on living is no newer.

Mine: In this life there's nothing hard in dying.
           To make one's life have meaning is much
           harder.

During my extensive work on the whole poem, I constantly thought of these lines. While working on other lines, I kept returning to these —consciously or unconsciously.[43]

Can we, to a certain extent, perform on Mayakovsky's article the same 'detective' work which revealed to us, behind Edgar Allan Poe's super-rational and objective mask of an analysis of his own 'The Raven', the essence of the true tangle of emotions which governed him while working on his poem?

Is there a second level here, a personal subtext beneath such a precisely and objectively expounded picture of 'how to make verse?'

Super-rationalizations always carry with them a suspicion of a certain Deck-Gebilde [masking image].

We saw to what extent Poe's emphasized rationalism served as a means of persuading others and, above all, himself, that he wrote the unusual and fantastic completely at will and not at all because, so he says, he was in the power of the irrational and controlled by it (as a result of the tragic aspects of a humiliating biography, alcoholism and use of opium, which there is full justification to suspect).

And it seems to me that in the case of Mayakovsky, too, there is a touch of this same thing.

Despite the fact that here, too, there is a certain (and, perhaps, first and foremost) 'obsessiveness' of this theme— although not of love, but of death—the greatness of Mayakovsky, however, lies in the fact that, while struggling with the spectre of death in its most cowardly aspect — the capacity to deprive oneself of one's own life—the poet leaves it not on the level of a personal matter and a night-time duel within an individual soul, but elevates this theme upon the material of a concrete occasion to the heights of generalization for the good of society and in order to break the ill-bearing wave which had started to spread from and because of the sad event of Sergei Esenin. (See, apart from Mayakovsky, the united speeches against this tide by the groups of organized Komsomols [Young Communists], literary figures and critics—speeches which were preserved in a number of special collections, dating from the anniversary of Esenin's catastrophe.)

For, however surprising and strange it may seem, the monolithic and stentorian Mayakovsky was not able to avoid many, many traits of the intelligentsia's neurasthenia in his own personality.

And the way in which he heroically surmounted and overcame them, turning everything into a matter of 'public service', does not at all lessen, but the opposite, heightens the importance of the individuality of this man who 'was and remains the best poet' of his and our time.[44]

Those who remember Mayakovsky on the stage could not help being struck by his amazing self-control, his brilliant wit, the relentless polemical mastery with which he felled his opponents right and left (opponents from both the Right and the Left!).

And how this belligerent image of a tribune does not coincide with the appearance of Mayakovsky backstage just before his speech—in such a degree of nervousness that only his staunch atheism, it would seem, supported him from crossing himself before coming out on to the stage, as especially nervous actresses do (something treacherously throwing their silhouette on the backdrop as they cross themselves backstage; I'll never forget that happening during a performance of Adrienne Lecouvreur in the Kamerny Theatre).[45]

Does an obsessive thought of death hover anywhere over the militant arsenal of his verse?

That would require the extraordinary laboriousness of an unproductive and even less generally useful work.

I shall recall, merely on the basis of my own living memory, an occasion when Mayakovsky was suddenly accused in my presence (during a speech in the Polytechnic Museum) of precisely this intelligentsia-like submissiveness to death as an outcome of his contradictions, by an absolutely unknown and not even young comrade in a leather jacket, who reproached him to his face, quoting— from a piece of paper—the lines about how 'the wheel of an engine will embrace' his neck.[46]

With his usual polemical fervour and mischief, the late Mayakovsky then pulverized his opponent with I no longer remember precisely what argument.

But the first thing that came to my mind when the news of Mayakovsky's tragic end reached me in Paris in 1930, was precisely this reproach by a quite ordinary reader of his, who, evidently possessing the keen ear of the new man of the rising class, had long before detected the sound of that motif which, over the years, was growing into one of the greatest tragedies of contemporary Russian literature.

There was much I could have recalled upon hearing this news, for I had met and encouraged Mayakovsky many times, starting with our first meeting back on Vodopyany Lane, through Lef and Novyi Lef, with which I broke,[47] through the later Sokolniki and Taganka theatres, if he is to be recalled on the basis of buildings, or the House of Scientists, the Polytechnic Museum, the Conservatory Hall, the Domino Club on Tverskaia Street, the building of the former Zone Theatre and the countless factory auditoriums, if you count on the basis of the stages, which were a unique chronology in his personal and militant biography.

But it was precisely this verse, read long ago in the Polytechnic Museum by some unknown person—with a crumpled paper in his hands—that immediately arose before me . . .

And from this point of view, the 'sobriety' (it is not accidental that this very word is so distinctly set off as a separate line)[48] of even individual passages of 'How To Make Verse', is heard all the more distinctly and admirably as a total subordination of personal theme to social theme, as a total removal of this personal theme from the framework of the article; an article which is wholly devoted to the question of single-minded service to one's class through verse and to a fascinating portrayal of how an aroused, ideological purpose blossoms into patterns and fractures of rhythm and is clothed in a system of verbal images.

The opinions I have set forth here are only meant to suggest an idea of the initial flood of emotion, from which later would be forged one of the greatest declaratory documents on the poet-citizen's service to society, a document deeply connected with a theme that is personal, tormenting, and tragic.

And the poet's greatness lies in the fact that his joy, suffering, and brilliant insight, together with the most tragic elements of psychological latency, are all clothed with equal inspiration in forcefully stentorian and resonant images, subjugated to the service of and in the interests of a common deed, a social command, unreserved service to his socialist country.

And both the profundity and passion of this work are constructed upon the fact that the personal, emotional theme is inseparably bound up with revolutionary consciousness, which transforms it into that intransient communal value, which the poem, To Sergei Esenin, constitutes in the general context of Mayakovsky's work.

••

Nowadays it is quite well known and demands no special proof that the qualitative distinction between an abnormal mind and a healthy mind is based upon a quantitative difference and extent of the presence of certain traits in one of them, as opposed to the other.

In this sense, data and observation of an abnormal mind help us identify elements of a healthy mind, which are present in these cases in an exaggerated form—as though under a microscope or magnifying glass.

The psychological mechanism, such as described by Juan Gris in relation to his own work, is sometimes present in yet greater intensity.

In such cases, it is connected with psychosis.

But the contours of the individual phases in this process preserve all the traits also found in the normal creative process.

Here—in the case of psychosis—it is merely as if they had been captured under a magnifying glass.

And then they no longer govern creative, imaginative activity on a canvas; they do not compromise a component of the creative will of a conscious artist, but hold in their power the will of a sick person, bound by obsessive ideas which intrude upon his everyday life, and which destroy the logic of his actions.

It would be possible to cite no few examples of this from the specialized literature on psychopathology.

We filmmakers, however, find ourselves in a very advantageous position in relation to this phenomenon.

Among the films of the last few years, there is one whose theme turns out to be precisely the story of a man controlled by obsessive ideas, and into the plot of the film is woven a portrayal of the method of psychotherapy, which in the end, helps him get well again. The phenomenon that interests us is presented in this film in the most popularized form.

And, therefore, instead of describing complex case histories from specialized works, we can take a similar case directly in the form as it is presented in this film.[49]

This film is Hitchcock's *Spellbound*.[50]

The only thing that interests me in this film at the moment is the line of action which is connected with the gradual explanation of the basic trauma of the hero through a series of various concrete images, through which he recalls the basic features of the situation connected with the origin of his psychosis.

In the presence of the hero, one of his interlocutors draws on a white tablecloth with a fork, explaining to him the layout of a park.

This drives the hero into a state of the most acute, nervous agitation.

While declaring his love to a girl, his eye catches hold of a pattern on her robe.

The robe is white with black stripes.

The hero is close to an attack.

He spends the night in the same room as her.

The blanket has black stripes against a white background.

In terrible agitation, he rushes into the bathroom.

Images of a white sink come at him.

A white chair.

A white table.

A white tub.

Grabbing a razor, he rushes out of the room.

The hero is calmed by a doctor.

He drinks a glass of milk.

The milk clouds the whole screen with white.

The patient loses consciousness.

During a doctor's consultation, snow falls outside the window.

The landscape outside the window is covered with a white blanket of snow.

The patients agitation increases.

One of the doctors look out the window and notices children riding sleds down a hill.

The sleds leave behind dark tracks from the runners. And eventually it is deciphered that the patient had received a psychological 'shock' while skiing with a different doctor who had treated him earlier.

During this outing, the doctor had been killed in an accident—by falling off a cliff (later it turns out that he had been shot from behind a tree by one of his enemies).

But in the patient's mind there comes to be formed, on the strength of a number of coincidental circumstances, the notion that he—the patient—is guilty of the doctor's death.

Under the influence of fear, the patient experiences, as a psychological displacement, a loss of memory of the actual circumstances of the accident that had frightened him.

As an escape from these frightening impressions, he suffers a total loss of memory, so-called amnesia.

Thus, he loses all memory of the real picture of the scene that had traumatized him.

There remains only a vague image of some abstracted, generalized elements of the strongest visual impression, remaining from the overall scene.

This is the track left by the darting skis upon the white blanket of snow.

Abstracted and generalized, it becomes simply a pattern of black lines traversing a white surface.

And, whatever particular, concrete forms this abstract pattern assumes, it always arouses the emotional shock which the scene itself had once produced on him.

This agitation, moreover, is so strong that the entire psychological mechanism is directed towards preventing any image of the real scene, which the consciousness and memory of the patient attempt to displace by any means, from becoming a distinct, conscious concept.

Whether this pattern of black lines against a white background materializes in the imprint of a fork upon a tablecloth, or in the form of black stripes on the surface of a white robe, as a black insert on a blanket, or black stripes of a shadow falling on a white bedspread, or even simply in white objects not crossed by anything—everywhere and always they evoke in the patient the same acute emotional agitation.

If we compare all this with what we cited from Juan Gris, we see that there is much in common here with the features of the psychological mechanism.

The only difference is the active, intentional tendentiousness and activity of the artist, as opposed to the passive subordination of the patient.

For the first—who elevated an arbitrary colour combination of two tones to a generalized thematic reading of it as a dramatic relationship—there is a wide open field of possibilities to actively convert this abstract correlation into realistically concrete and imagistic embodiments.

For the second—the patient—who is constrained, entranced (which is what spellbound literally means) by a specific trauma remaining in the consciousness as a vague image of its characteristic colour traits—any object that coincidentally possesses the same correlation of colours is emotionally equated with the original impressions that disturbed him.

I once cited Diderot in this regard, as one who already knew of this phenomenon (from letters to Madame Volland—see 'Vertical Montage', second article).[51]

In all other respects both of these three-phase processes resemble each other in terms of their basic pattern.

With the artist—making every allowance for Gris' one-sidedness—we have: an actual colour impression— an abstracted colour generalized to the degree of thematic significance—and a new embodiment in a series of new colour objects or vehicles.

With the patient: an actual colour impression from a concrete scene—a remaining colour generalization reduced to a pattern, which is capable of reflexively evoking the entire emotional complex connected with the original situation—an emotional complex that arises on contact with any concrete object that coincidentally possesses the same trait of linear-colour correlations.

In comparing the two, the communality, as well as the qualitative difference of both cases, become completely apparent.

The most interesting thing, however, is the fact that the same three-phase process with the very same features occurs in yet another portion of mental activity.

From the three-phase process in the form as it occurs in the work of an artist, we have only glanced to the left, as it were—in one direction from it—in the direction of those cases when the harmonic balance of the interaction between the emotional and rational sources in the artist is upset towards a prevalence of the irrational. Here, we unavoidably ran up against, and had to run up against, psychosis—the forms taken on by our three-phase process in the conditions of . . . madness.

I shall not try to glance, as it were, to the right—in the direction where the rational source starts to prevail.

This realm, naturally, will prove to be the sphere, not of imagistic and artistic creation, but of an activity no less creative—intellectual activity.

And again, our very same three-phase pattern proves to underlie the coming into being of this activity as well.

Perhaps in yet a new qualitative aspect, but with all its basic traits in precisely the same form as we outlined above.

About the fact that it is precisely such, we have at our disposal the most authoritative data.

About intellectual activity, about cognition and about approaching truth, writes Lenin:

> Thought proceeding from the concrete to the abstract—provided it is correct—does not get away from the truth but comes closer to it. The abstraction of matter, of a law of nature, the abstraction of value, etc., in short all scientific (correct, serious, not absurd) abstractions reflect nature more deeply, truly and completely. From living perception to abstract thought, and from this to practice—such is the dialectical path of the cognition of truth, of the cognition of objective reality.[52]

Commenting upon the second of these ideas concerning the question of theoretical and practical thought, Boris Teplov writes:

> The work of the theoretical mind is concentrated primarily upon the first portion of the whole course of cognition: the transition from living perception to abstract thought, the (temporary)

departure or digression from practice. The work of the practical mind is concentrated chiefly upon the second part of this course of cognition: the transition from abstract thought to practice, the same sure fire leap towards practice, for which the 'theoretical departure' is also made.[53]

(The reference here is yet to another of Lenin's statements: 'The movement of cognition to the object can always only proceed dialectically: to retreat in order to hit more surely—*reculer pour mieux sauter* (*savoir?*) . . .')[54]

As we see, not only is the general pattern here of the successive phases absolutely the same as in the cases we described, but here too—in intellectual activity—its individual varieties are also present, depending upon which phase of the overall process is more or less accented.

We see, therefore, that the method we sensed in working with colour in creative practice, adheres wholly to the very same set of laws governing human practice, including such serious and crucial realms as intellectual activity—and in both of its most distinct manifestations: theoretical and practical thought.

NOTES

1   The three sections that make up this article were written
    by E for his unfinished book *Colour* (1946-8). When
    Colour was published in *IP3* (1964), the editors decided
    to omit these three sections because they seemed to
    digress too far from the discussion of colour proper.
    Colour examined the process by which artists in different
    media select the colours they use for a given work: the
    banquet sequence in the second part of *Ivan the Terrible*,
    the paintings of Pablo Picasso and Juan Gris, the poetry
    of Alexander Blok, are discussed in terms of the the-
    matic role played by colour in these works. The sections
    published here serve as a kind of introduction to this
    discourse, demonstrating how the choice of a theme is
    itself dictated by the same psychological processes that
    also govern the artist's choice of colours. E wrote the
    section on Edgar Allan Poe on 4–5 February 1947; the
    fragment on Mayakovsky followed a few days later;
    the section on *Spellbound* is dated 17 April 1947. The
    original Seagull Books publication in 1987 marked the
    first appearance of this essay: it was translated from a
    typescript provided by Naum Kleiman, from the
    Eisenstein Cabinet in Moscow.

2 (E's note) It should be borne in mind that Juan Gris was close to the well-known mathematician Maurice Princet, and through his mathematically inclined mind, he significantly influenced the mathematical element within Cubism. This, however, in no way hindered the expansiveness and licence of his imagination or his flights of fancy.

[Editor's note] Juan Gris (1887–1927) was a Spanish painter closely involved in the Cubist movement. Maurice Princet was a Frenchman with an interest in mathematics, who made his living as a financial actuary, but whose enthusiasm for notions of time as the fourth spatial dimension and friendship with Gris made him an important catalyst in spreading ideas similar to Einstein's theory of relativity to the artistic avant-garde. Princet is sometimes credited with having influenced Picasso's painting, *Les Demoiselles d'Avignon*.

3 Juan Gris, 'Système esthéthique . . . Méthode', *Esprit nouveau* 5 (February 1921): 533–4, cited in: D. H. Kahnweiler, *Juan Gris: His Life and Work*, (D. Cooper trans.) (London: Lund Humphries, 1947), p. 138.

4 Edgar Allan Poe (1809–49), American poet and short-story writer, whom E often cited for his examples.

5 In *Colour*, E defines the correct use of colour in art as a three-phase process: (1) Colour is separated form an object. (2) Colour is 're-worked'—given an emotional or dramatic function dictated by the themes. (3) Colour is 're-materialized'—in concrete objects or details, again dictated by the theme. Thus arise 'colour images', capable of expressing ideas. E saw Gris's work as stopping short of this final phase (*IP3*, p. 543): 'Juan Gris halts

at the threshold of possibilities of raising colour images —as the vehicles of meaning and idea—and limits himself to making these abstract colour elements take on the appearance of objects, without any attempt to include them in the structure of thematic meaning.'

6   H. H. Ewers (1871–1943), German poet and novelist. E is referring to his book *Edgar Allan Poe* [1905]. References in the current volume are to the English translation: *Edgar Allan Poe* (A. Lewisohn trans.) (New York: B. W. Huebsch, 1917).

7   Edgar Allan Poe, 'The Balloon-Hoax' (1844) in *Poetry and Tales* (New York: Library of America, 1984), p. 743.

(E's note) Another historical example of a similar—this time, theatrical, 'hoax', is the not-unknown feuilleton by Jules Janin, who, in a single day through one article in Le Figaro, created from an unknown cabotin of the cheap little Théâtre des Funambules, a figure of ever-lasting and immortal glory.

Many years later, the querulous Sarcey disapprovingly described the history of this 'scandalous hoax' which had been intentionally perpetrated by the then all-powerful 'king of the feuilleton for the express purpose of mocking the public. The fashion created was truly unheard of, but the most amusing part of all was that the central image of this 'hoax' actually proved to be a stupendous and amazing artist of pantomime . . . Deburau!

[Editor's note] Jules-Gabriel Janin (1804–74) was a French literary and dramatic critic whose collected essays and reviews were published in six volumes as *Histoire de la littérature dramatique* (1858). Francisque

Sarcey (1827–99) was a French dramatic critic and historian. The source E alludes to has not been identified. Jean-Gaspard Deburau (1796–1846) was the Bohemian-born French mime and star of the Théâtre des Funambules from 1820 until his death, who developed the secondary character of Pierrot into a pale, elongated hero of mythic proportions. He was reincarnated as Baptiste, played by Jean-Louis Barrault, in Marcel Carné's film *Les Enfants du Paradis* [France, 1945].

8   J. W. Krutch, *Edgar Allan Poe: A Study in Genius* (New York: Alfred A. Knopf, 1926), p. 113. Krutch visited the Soviet Union in the late 1920s as a theatre critic, at which time he conducted an interview with E; 'The Season in Moscow (III): Eisenstein and Lunacharsky', *The Nation* (27 June 1928).

9   Reference to M. Bonaparte, *Edgar Poe, étude psychoanalytique* (Paris: Denoël et Steele, 1933).

10 (E's note) See the same thing even in the novel *Busman's Honeymoon* by such an outstanding specialist as Dorothy Sayers, who applies the method of scientific detection even to biblical situations, establishing, for example, how and in what circumstances the stone was moved aside from the cave containing the tomb of Christ (in the notes to her radio adaptation of the life of Christ—*The Man Born to Be King*.

[Editor's note] Dorothy L. Sayers, *Busman's Holiday: A Love Story with Detective Interruptions* (New York: Harper & Row, 1937); Dorothy L. Sayers, *The Man Born to Be King: A Play-Cycle on the Life of our Lord and Saviour Jesus Christ, Written for Broadcasting* (New York: Harper, 1948).

11 Edgar Allan Poe, 'The Philosophy of Composition' in *Essays and Reviews* (New York: Library of America, 1984), p. 15.

12 ibid., pp. 15–17.

13 Reference to the poem 'The Stranger' [Neznakomka, 1907] by Alexander Blok (1880–1921), which he discusses at greater length in *Colour* in: *IP4*, pp. 559–67.

14 The 'starry sisterhood' was the name given to New York's women literati, whose salons Poe frequented. The citation is from: Harvey Allen, *Israfel: The Life and Times of Edgar Allan Poe* (New York: Farrar & Rinehart, 1934), p. 524. E appears to have drawn most of his biographical data from this source.

15 *The Best Known Works of Edgar Allan Poe* (New York: Blue Ribbon Books, 1925).

16 (E's note) I have dwelt upon these details, not only because we needed a brief background about Lenore, but also because certain motifs in To Helen recall the poems of Blok, which we shall analyse later (and the very persistence of the theme of Lenore recalls in its own way Blok's The Stranger, which we shall also discuss).

This story of young love for Mrs Stanard will come to mind when we start to explain the dramatic colour construction of the scenario on Pushkin, the plot of which is based on the conception underlying Tynyanov's *A Nameless Love*.

[Editor's note] One of E's many unrealized projects was 'The Love of a Poet'—a plan conceived by him in 1940 for a colour film on the life of Alexander Pushkin. See: Jay Leyda and Zina Voynow, *Eisenstein at Work* (New York: Pantheon Books, 1982), pp. 116–22; *ESW4*, pp.

712–24. E's script borrowed an idea from the article by Yuri N. Tynyanov which suggested that the source of inspiration for Pushkin's greatest works was his 'nameless love' for Ekaterina A. Karamzin (1780–1851), the wife of his friend and literary mentor, the famous Russian historian Nikolai M. Karamzin (1766–1826). See: Iu. Tynianov, 'Bezymennaia liubov', *Literaturnyi kritik* 5–6 (May–June 1939): 160–80.

17 Una Pope-Hennessy, *Edgar Allan Poe, 1809–49: A Critical Biography* (London: Macmillan, 1934), p. 148.

18 (E's note) An inclination towards endless repetition is extremely characteristic for all highly ecstatic creators. Just as repetition plays the decisive role in forms of ecstatic trances, so in the works of such artists do we observe it in endlessly repeated works.

It is sufficient to recall El Greco's countless repetitions of the very same forms throughout the various subjects, the endless variations on the very same themes and the simple repetitions of previously painted pictures, with what seems to be merely a change of colour spectrum within their plastic composition (about which we wrote earlier).

[Editors' note] E analyses El Greco's paintings in *NIN*, pp. 112–23, 359–62; cf. *ESW2*, pp. 345–7; *ESW4*, pp. 300–06, 462–3.

19 Poe, 'Philosophy', p. 13.

20 Dante Gabriel Rossetti (1828–82), English painter and poet and in 1848 one of the founding members of the Pre-Raphaelite Brotherhood. He married the beautiful but sickly Elizabeth Siddall, the subject of many of his most famous images, in 1860 and, when she died two

years later, he placed the only complete manuscript of his poems in her coffin. He was persuaded to have them exhumed in 1869 and they were published the following year.

21 Reference to Pushkin's 'little tragedy' *Mozart and Salieri* [1830]: 'Killing the sounds, I dissected music like a corpse'. See: Alexander Pushkin, *The Bronze Horseman and Other Poems* (D. M. Thomas trans.) (Harmondsworth: Penguin, 1982), p. 148.

22 Ewers, *Edgar Allan Poe*, p. 23.

23 (E's note) We must not forget that the word 'decomposition' (both in Russian and in the German—Zersetzung—as well as in English) embraces two forms—both active and passive, uniting both the author's urge to act and that which happens to the dead.

24 Pope-Hennessy, *Edgar Allan Poe*, p. 203.

25 Reference to the drag bars and cabarets that E is reputed to have visited on one of his visits to the German capital in the years 1926–30.

26 Frances Keeling Allan was Poe's foster-mother.

27 In a letter written in 1943 to Yuri Tynyanov but never posted, E compared the notorious 'Don Juanism' of both Chaplin and Pushkin:

> The sentimental biography of Chaplin, with whom I became quite close, was precisely such.
>
> This was his love for the very same Marion Davies (not to be confused with Bette Davis), who was 'devoted to another'—to Randolph Hearst (the newspaperman) and,

even without any observance of formal church conventions or civil ceremonies.

Hearst was the same chastising Vater imago [father image] as Karamzin, only in much more frightening and noisy form, who almost crushed Chaplin to death once during one of Chaplin's 'recurrences' of amorous outbursts towards Marion Davies . . .

In either event, how amusing: Randolph Hearst and Karamzin, Mrs Karamzin and Marion, Pushkin—Chaplin.

Source: *Iurii Tynianov: pisatel' i uchenyi* [Yuri Tynyanov: Writer and Scholar] (Moscow: Molodaia gvardiia, 1966), p. 178.

28 Poe, 'Philosophy', pp. 14–15.

29 Poe, 'Philosophy', p. 15.

30 Poe, 'Philosophy', p. 17.

31 Poe, 'Philosophy', pp. 18–19.

32 Poe, 'Philosophy', pp. 18–19.

33 Lenore had actually been written in 1831.

34 Poe, Poetry and Tales, p. 68.

35 Poe, 'Philosophy', p. 14.

36 (E's note) Father Ronald Knox, in his introductory article to a collection of the best detective stories of 1928–29, while enumerating the 'commandments' of the detective genre, places this condition under a number [gap in ms]: 'Ellery Queen, a collective pseudonym of two authors [Frederic Dannay and Manfred B. Lee], makes a rule of halting the narrative at the very moment when the reader has all the information in his hands,

and of warning the reader with a special challenge that, from that moment on, he knows just as much as the detective and can himself solve the mystery.

[Editors' note] Upchurch had to translate this quotation back from the Russian because the source cited by E has not been traced. The famous 'commandments' of the detective genre were first set forth by the writer and priest, Ronald Arbuthnott Knox (1888–1957) in 1924. Knox's essay went through several revisions. Cf. his introduction to *The Best Detective Stories of the Year 1928* (London: Faber & Gwyer, 1929); Ronald Arbuthnott Knox, 'Detective Stories' in *Literary Distractions* (New York: Sheed & Ward, 1958). But none coincides with E's citation. It seems likely that he has confused his sources.

37 Poe, 'Philosophy', p. 20.

38 Poe, 'Philosophy', p. 20.

39 Elizabeth Barrett Browning (1806–61), English poet.

40 (E's note) The dedication: 'To the Noblest of her Sex, the author of *The Drama in Exile*—to Miss Elizabeth Barrett of England.'

[Editors' note] See *The Complete Poems of Edgar Allan Poe* (L. Untermeyer ed.) (New York: Heritage Press, 1943), p. 100.

41 'To Sergei Esenin' [Sergeiu Eseninu, 1926] was Mayakovsky's indignant response to the 'senseless suicide' of one of Russia's most beloved poets, Sergei A. Esenin (1895–1925). See: Vladimir Mayakovsky, *Poems* (D. Rottenberg trans.) (Moscow, Progress, 1972), pp. 88–93.

42 Esenin hanged himself on 26 December 1925. His 'suicide poem', written in his own blood 24 hours earlier, was first published in the Leningrad newspaper *Krasnaia gazeta* on 29 December 1925. For a translation of this poem and a discussion of the controversy surrounding Esenin's death, see: Gordon McVay, *Esenin: A Life* (Ann Arbor, MI: Ardis, 1976).

43 Vladimir Mayakovsky, *How to Make Verse* (V. Coe trans.) (Willimantic, CT: Curbstone, 1985), pp. 41, 48–9, 51–2, 57, 58, 81–2.

44 In 1936, six years after Mayakovsky's suicide, his mistress Lily Brik wrote to Stalin complaining that his work was no longer published. In his reply, Stalin used the remark cited here and went on to say that 'indifference to his memory and his works is a crime'. The writer Boris Pasternak commented that Stalin's endorsement was Mayakovsky's 'second death' and that his work was subsequently forcibly introduced 'like potatoes under Catherine the Great'. See: E. J. Brown, *Mayakovsky: A Poet in the Revolution* (Princeton NJ: Princeton University Press, 1973), p. 370.

45 *Adrienne Lecouvreur* [1849], a play by Eugène Scribe and Gabriel Legouvé, based on the life of the 17th-century actress of the Comédie Française.

46 This is the final line of the prologue to Mayakovsky's drama in verse, *Vladimir Mayakovsky: A Tragedy* [1913]. See: Vladimir Mayakovsky, *Electric Iron* (J. Hirschmann and V. Erlich trans.) (Berkeley, CA: Maya, 1971).

47 *Lef* [1923–25] and *Novyi Lef* [1927–28] were journals co-founded by Mayakovsky. E's article 'The Montage of Attractions' was published in *Lef* 3 (1923).

48 E is referring to the opening lines of Mayakovsky's poem 'To Sergei Esenin' (*Poems*, p. 88):

> You've departed,
> as they say,
> to another world.
> Emptiness ...
> Fly on,
> with stars colliding.
> No money to collect.
> No beershops.
> In a word—
> Sobriety.

49 (E's note) For those who are acquainted with the film itself, this will have the added advantage of being a reference to familiar material.

50 *Spellbound* [USA, 1945] was directed by Alfred Hitchcock (1899–1980). The film starred Ingrid Bergman and Gregory Peck and the dream sequences were designed by the Spanish Surrealist artist, Salvador Dalí (1904–89).

51 *ESW2*, pp. 362–3.

52 V. I. Lenin, *Philosophical Notebooks* in *Collected Works*, VOL. 38 (Moscow: Foreign Languages Publishing House, 1961), p. 171.

53 B. M. Teplov, 'K voprosu o prakticheskom myshlenii' [On the Question of Practical Thought] in *Psikhologiia: dvizhenie i deiatel'nost'* [Psychology: Movement and Activity], *Uchennye zapiski MGU* [Moscow State University Learned Papers], VOL. 90 (Moscow: MGU, 1945), p. 150.

54 Lenin, *Philosophical Notebooks*, pp. 279–80.

ON THE DETECTIVE STORY[1]

Do we dare suggest that the laws of effective composition of plots, as an element of form, follow the same laws as other varieties of form?

Can we, for example, suggest that the methods and laws of the trope also have a place in the composition of the actions and events of a situation or plot?

We shall see.

There is a very old story about a peasant and eyeglasses.

A peasant goes into an optician's shop.

He wants to buy some glasses.

He tries on a pair.

He is given a page of printed text to read.

He cannot make it out.

He is given another pair of glasses.

He cannot make it out.

A third pair.

Same thing.

The fitting continues.

But with no success.

It turns out that the peasant has perfect vision, but he is illiterate.

And against this ailment, glasses are powerless.

Another example.

Even in my earlier youth, I was crazy about the endless series of crime-detective novels, which had as their hero the elusive Fantômas.[2]

A contemporary of the film serial about Irma Vep (*Les Vampires*),[3] it captivated the imagination and caused one's blood to freeze at moments when a huge black boa constrictor would slither into a tightly barricaded room through the aperture of a radiator, crushing in its grip a helpless victim; or when Lady Beltham's secret lover, Fantômas, would escape through a wall at the very moment when the indefatigable detective Juve grabbed him tightly by the arm: his glove, made from a murdered man's skin, would come off, and Fantômas' arm would slip freely away . . .

Fantômas was so popular well into the NEP years that this intriguing and magnificent name adorned a cinema on the corner of Sretenka and Boulevard Ring A [in Moscow].

In distant Mexico. Many, many years later, in some provincial hole of one of the most desolate states, where we had been drawn in a search for the untouched purity of tropical bird colonies and flat stingray fish resembling deflated balloons, I had to watch in a single night, in a single showing, a hodgepodge of the entire *Fantômas* serial, shredded into unrecognisable tatters of what were once the films.

All around me sat uncomprehending bronzed faces. They had come to this stuffy dark oven for a completely different reason. The squeals coming from the darkness revealed their intentions. While on the screen, the formerly glorious and proud epic of the legendary villain stumbled along in fits and starts. There was the glistening black surface of the boa constrictor. There were the detectives who had surrounded the villain and grabbed him by the shoulders, left in disbelief with a cape and a pair of rubber arms in their hands while the hero slipped away from under the cape in his tail-coat. There they were, jerking back their hands as they tried to grab him under the arms, pricked on the spiked steel bracelets hidden under his elegant cuffs … Neither interest nor excitement around. These snatches of film said nothing to my neighbours. They reminded them of nothing. But my neighbours in the dark were not wasting their time. Their girlfriends continued their frenzied squealing.

That was probably my last encounter with the dominant influence on my youth.

Prior to that, I had had another. In Paris. One much more exciting and joyful.

I had gone hunting for a complete set of this immortal creation of Pierre Souvestre and Marcel Allain. It consists of thirty-two volumes of 400 pages each.

The *Iliad* consisted of only twenty-four songs.

I rummaged for hours in *bouquinistes'* boxes, which stretched along the embankment the length of the silvery Seine, just as *bouquiniste* stands once lined the wall of our Chinatown.[4]

Neither the wall, nor the stands remain.[5]

The reconstruction of Moscow has done away with both.

Do those Parisian banks of the Seine still look the same, cloaked in Romanticism, as they will forever live in the memories of bibliophiles and lovers of book *curiosa?*

Or have they, too, been swept away by Hitler's Fascist boots?

It was from this embankment that I carried to my little hotel in the Montparnasse a pile of old books. Runs of Rochefort's *La Lanterne*.[6] A history of the Théâtre des Funambules, where the immortal Deburau had performed.[7] And a nearly complete set of *Fantômas*. The set sparkled with a fantastic array of colourful covers: a furious shoot-out over an open grave between two men dressed as nuns in wide, white habits;[8] a man crawling out of the fountain on the Place de la Concorde, formerly the site of the guillotine, but in the novel, concealing a secret underwater room where Fantômas imprisons a certain king;[9] another (under the colourful title, *The Hempen Collar*)[10] shows a Russian priest holding last rites for two figures behind him bound tightly to chairs. Turning this cover over, we learn that Fantômas once killed and assumed the identity of the chief of the Secret Police in St Petersburg, and that part of his Russian adventures take place in Gatchina, 'a poor little fishing village' on the shores of the severe Gulf of Finland.[11] In this novel, Juve's enterprising friend, the journalist Fandor, stops the Trans-Siberian Express at full speed by greasing the rails with a barrel of . . . green soap that had accidentally fallen from a freight train.

The set was lacking the volume with the spectre of Fantômas in a black mask and, of course tail coat, floating over Paris and tramping the fire-engulfed city underfoot;[12] and also the one where the horrible severed hand in the black glove lies upon a roulette table, surrounded by gold and banknotes.[13]

But let us stop this stream of lyric outpourings and instead describe a scene from one of these colourful novels that I am now thinking of.

In a setting of mysterious and nightmarish crimes involving disappearing corpses and the like, the local idiot runs into a village police station.[14]

While wandering through the woods, he had stumbled upon a secluded villa. Its front door was open.

He walked through the rooms.

Went into the bathroom.

An incredibly beautiful woman was taking a bath.

The idiot reached out his hand to touch her.

But the lady bit him on the finger, and the idiot ran off yelping.

Later we discover that:

there was no lady taking a bath.

It was a corpse in the bathtub, the very one that later disappeared.

And it was not water at all that was in the tub.

But nitric acid, which had been used to dispose of the body.

And what the poor idiot had thought was a bite, was nothing other than a burn from this same acid.

Later, Fantômas would also dispose of this witness, irresponsible though he was, to his dark machinations in a very colourful fashion.

But let us forget about Fantômas and concern ourselves with the situation described.

It is quite clear that the structure of the episode is absolutely the same as that of the peasant and the eyeglasses.

But what name should we give this type of comic or dramatic situation?

It seems to me we can include it, with full justification, in the category of 'plot metonymy'.

Let us recall its definition:

[*Metonymy*. A figure of speech which consists in substituting for the name of a thing the name of an attribute of it or of something closely related.][15]

I believe that both our examples fit wholly within this definition.

No one is likely to disagree, but an objection could be made that we are dealing here with material that is non-canonical and extremely specific.

Let us take some more examples.

Once, when I was following quite a different line of research involving folk tales about Ivan the Terrible, I stumbled upon the article, 'Folk Tales about Ivan the Terrible' (1876) in the 16th volume of A. N. Veselovsky's *Collected Works*.

Among them was a tale about Shibarsha.

It was about [Ivan] the Terrible's attempt to catch a thief.

Tsar Ivan lured Shibarsha's uncle into a cauldron of boiling pitch and burned him alive. In order to catch Shibarsha himself,

Tsar Ivan Vasilevich ordered the dead man's body to be dragged through the streets of Moscow; whoever gasped or grieved at the sight would be seized, for he would be the thief.

Shibarsha asked his aunt: did she want to weep for is uncle? If so, then to take a pitcher of milk and walk past the body.

'The soldiers will start pushing you away from him. Drop the pitcher and start crying, as if because of the pitcher, and say to them: "I'll bring charges against you for this; why did you break my pitcher of milk?"'

And that is what the woman did: not only did she manage to mourn for her husband, she also received ten roubles from the soldiers so as not to press charges. And so the thief went uncaught.[16]

It is perfectly clear that this example belongs here as well.

In this regard, one more point should be taken into consideration.

The point is not simply the plot metonymy of its structure, but also the metonymy, well known as a method of early mentality, is introduced here as a deliberate, clever trick.

As though 'falling back' to the norm of an earlier method of thinking enables a clever man to outwit those who have already progressed to the logical level.

Now you start looking for other examples in possible support of this thesis, no longer as an isolated exception, but as something common and essential to this type of construction.

An example is found right next to it in Shibarsha's next trick.

Shibarsha manages to outwit Tsar Ivan once more.

Assuming that Shibarsha cannot resist the sight of gold, Ivan Vasilevich orders gold coins to be scattered throughout the taverns. Whoever bends down to pick up the coins is to be seized: it would be the thief Shibarsha.

Shibarsha outwits him again.

He smears the soles of his boots with pitch:

The gold sticks to them.

But Shibarsha has too much to drink and falls asleep.

The soldiers notice the gold on Shibarsha's soles.

They shave off half of the sleeping man's hair and beard so as to be able to identify him in the morning.

But Shibarsha wakes up earlier than the rest and shaves them all in the same way.

They cannot identify or find Shibarsha.[17]

An identical example occurs in an Egyptian story about Rhampsinitus, which, incidentally, was retold by Heinrich Heine.[18] Here the king's daughter smears black dye on the young man, one of a number sleeping in the same room with her, who dared try to make love to her. Rhampsinitus luckily wakes up, notices this, and, precisely like Shibarsha, smears dye on all the others![19]

We see that in this case as well, both Shibarsha and Rhampsinitus perform the same 'regressive' operation: they return an individual unit that has been separated from the undifferentiated 'sum total', back to the undivided whole of exact equals.

And again the higher categories of reason are disgraced.

Two examples—that is already noteworthy.

But let us take yet a third case from a situation which we analysed earlier on the basis of its material.[20] For the trick with which Portia wins her trial against Shylock is constructed on the very same thing. When she demands a precise definition of the term 'a pound of flesh'—not one ounce more or less than a pound—she essentially performs a reverse displacement of the general concept of a pound to a concrete unit of measure.

When Chatsky says, 'a million torments', no one thinks that he has 999,999 torments plus one.[21]

Or when Hamlet says he loved Ophelia like 'forty thousand brothers' could not love, again he means the amount (degree) of his love, and not the literal strength of the love of 39,999 brothers plus one!

Likewise we say 'a thousand pardons' and 'how are you?' But our interlocutors would be extremely surprised if we took it into our head to factually enumerate ten hundred phrases of pardon, just as we would be no less surprised to hear in reply, not a short 'fine, thank you', but a detailed picture of his life and experiences.

The question here of a pound of flesh is very pointed, for 'a pound of flesh' is simply a conventional formula, a figure of speech in which lurks the idea of killing (which was a form of punishing insolvent debtors permitted by ancient legal codes) . . .

In her speech, Portia returns the figurative concept of a pound of flesh, 'killing', back to the initial, primary, concrete stage. This is known as a reversion to the norms of 'concrete' thought. We encountered this earlier in the example of Natasha Rostova at the opera.[22] We also recalled the comic effect of this confusion achieved by Swift in his humorous description of the Laputan scientists.[23]

And so in all three cases, it is the 'back of the mind' that gains the upper hand: behaviour and interpretation made in the norms of early and sensuous thought.

The same ironic blow to 'common sense' is struck here in terms of practice, plot, situation, in the play of 'circumstances', such as Engels ridiculed (see the earlier section on refusal of movement).[24]

The notorious 'native wit' in folk wisdom is based on this.

For in the well-known folk tale of the three questions posed by the Tsar to a sexton, disguised as a priest, a sly, cunning person once again gets out of a difficult situation by means of the very same manoeuvre.

When the Tsar asks: 'What am I thinking?'

The disguised one answers: 'You're thinking a priest stands before you, but I'm a sexton!'

Again a displacement from a generalized concept of the content of thoughts to the literal-objective.

The 'philosophy' behind this trick is, no doubt, quite profound.

I believe it is based on a disapproval of the alienation of common sense that has been elevated, intellectualized from the depths of folk wisdom, from the reliable gains of practical experience entirely in the direction of superficial, facile, and hasty deductions.

A deficit of the sensuous, pre-logical component, which, equally with formally differentiating logic, makes up a constituent part of absolute or dialectical thought, has been condemned, as we see, since time immemorial. These tales about native wit and folk wisdom contain the same reminder of the vitality only of that which is deeply connected with folkness in its roots, such as is also present in a number of rituals.

Thus in the past, Czech kings were buried on top of oxen, after having wooden peasant shoes placed on their feet.

This served to remind the heir to the throne that the king comes from the people.

My reasoning is supported by a certain ancient custom, a recollection of which runs through one of the most popular, traditional situations (and which, incidentally, is also found in the drama that linked Shylock with Portia).

I am thinking of the ritual test in ancient India when priests were ordained, according to the Upanishads or Vedas.

As the data of these historical sources testify, the initiate into the priesthood was asked—riddles.

Why?

I think there is only one answer here.

What is there in the nature of a riddle that distinguishes it from a 'solution'?

The difference is that a solution gives the name of an object as a formulation, whereas a riddle presents the same object in the form of an image woven from a certain number of its attributes.

The degree to which the attributes are characteristic, while still remaining difficult to solve, makes the riddle high style, as opposed to a comic riddle which purposely selects that which is incidental, uncharacteristic or even contradictory. A riddle like: 'What has fur all around and cotton inside?' Answer: 'A dog running round a pharmacy.'

Or 'What is it that cannot be seen from the top, from the bottom, or from the sides?' Answer: 'A watermelon inside a box.' Compare these with such wonderful models of folk riddles as: 'What has a hole on the top, a hole on the bottom, and fire and water inside?' 'A samovar.' Or the well-known three riddles of the Sphinx.

Why must a priest be able to solve riddles?

The point is certainly not the riddles themselves.

But rather to make certain that he who has been initiated into the great mysteries has also been initiated to an equal and identical degree into:

the speech of ideas,

the speech of imagistic concepts,

the language of logic,

and the language of feelings.

The degree of comprehension while approaching unity and mutual penetration is an indication of the degree to which the initiation already comprehends absolute, dialectical thought. Not yet materialist, for this was not yet historically possible in such ancient conditions. But there were already the rudiments of dialectics in India, just as there were in China or Greece.

It is highly unusual to ransack these early stages for elaborations of concepts.

Sketch made by Eisenstein, *En filature* (Trailing) on 30 September 1944
(Eisenstein Cabinet).

Welcoming reception for visiting Japanese writers at the All-Union Society
for Cultural Relations with Foreign Countries (VOKS), Moscow, 1924.
LEFT TO RIGHT: Boris Pasternak, Eisenstein, Olga Treyakova, Lily Brik,
Vladimir Mayakovsky. (Eisenstein Cabinet)

Cover illustrations by Gino Starace to the first editions of *Fantômas*
(1911–13).

Cover illustrations by Gino Starace to the first editions of *Fantômas*
(1911–13).

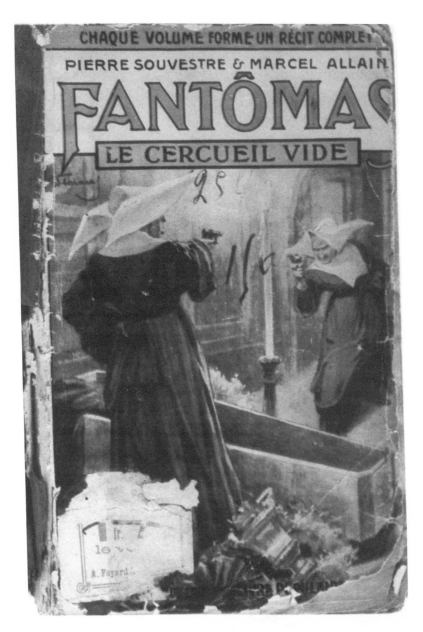

Cover illustrations by Gino Starace to the first editions of *Fantômas*
(1911–13).

Shoot-out among the wine-barrels at the Bercy warehouse, from
Louis Feuillade's 1913 *Juve contre Fantômas* (Museum of Modern Art
/ Film Stills Archives).

The lair of Moscow's criminal underworld, from Eisenstein's 1924 film
The Strike. (Eisenstein Cabinet)

TOP: The many disguises of Fantômas, from *Juve contre Fantômas* (Museum of Modern Art/Film Stills Archives).

BOTTOM: Spies hired to infiltrate workers' secret meetings, from *The Strike*. (Eisenstein Cabinet)

A sketch made by Eisenstein in Alma-Ata on 30 December 1943, illus-
trating a scene from G. K. Chesterton's story, 'The Blue Cross', in *The
Innocence of Father Brown*. (Eisenstein Cabinet)

But a condescending haughtiness towards their naïveté or imperfection is wholly uncalled for here.

It is far more interesting to trace the roots and germs of later thought formations, which only at our stage attained total clarity.

In all such cases, I fondly recall Engels' similar words concerning the Utopians:

> These new social systems were foredoomed as Utopian; the more completely they were worked out in detail, the more they could not avoid drifting off into pure phantasies.
>
> These facts once established, we need not dwell a moment longer upon this side of the question, now wholly belonging to the past. We can leave it to the literary small fry to solemnly quibble over these phantasies, which today only make us smile, and to crow over the superiority of their own bald reasoning, as compared with such 'insanity'. For ourselves, we delight in the stupendously grand thoughts and germs of thought that everywhere break out through their phantastic covering, and to which these Philistines are blind.[25]

It is no accident that the solver of riddles is usually also invested with the great power of deciding fates.

For he knows the very secret of the movement and coming into being of phenomena of nature.

From this stage of the 'priestly test', the riddle later develops into a traditional plot condition in the folk tale, myth, epos, and drama.

And always the riddle remains, first and foremost, an essential test of the integrity of the mind, which has mastered all layers and overcome all 'depths'.

An artist works precisely the same way in the realm of form, but solves his riddle in a directly opposite manner.

An artist is 'given' a solution—a conceptually formulated thesis—and his job is to make of it . . . a 'riddle'; i.e. to put it in imagistic form.

To figure out from his 'solution'—how to answer a 'riddle'. This substitution of a precise definition by a vague, imagistic description of attributes is preserved as a method in literature.

For example, what is not a 'riddle', in our sense, of a description such as: 'The most precious of all man's acquisitions, a proud and passionate beast.'

True, in this particular case, one cannot but agree with d'Alembert, who reproached Buffon for this style and said to La Harpe: 'Why not simply say a horse?' (according to Pushkin's well-known remark).[26]

What deserves condemnation here, of course, is not the method itself, but the excessiveness and inappropriateness of its application; i.e. for cases when one needs 'to explain the most ordinary, simple things'. Nonetheless, in the method of art and in proper measure, it is just as Goethe said: 'My task is the embodiment of ideas.' ('Meine Tendenz ist die Verkörperung der Ideen.')[27]

This is what ancient Hindu epic did.

Heine laments the fact that the keys to its solutions are lost, and is fully justified in supposing it to be a great depository of ancient wisdom, shrouded in the form of a grandiose riddle.

That is how Spinoza viewed the epos of the Bible.

It would be wrong to suppose that the contents of these books had been 'arbitrarily' encoded by means of imagistic speech.

They were written at a time when sensuous-imagistic expressions were the only ones available at that stage of development.

All the more reason why the wise man and the priest must be able to 'read' this ancient, former, imagistic-sensuous speech and master not only the younger speech of logic!

From here, no doubt, also comes that strange circumstance that the wisest of all turns out to be the fool. For of course in terms of the norms of 'common sense', a creature who possesses the mysteries of the 'back of the mind' cannot be otherwise.

Furthermore: the contents of the victory of this form of thought are wholly in the sphere of that primal, practically applied cunning, about which Marx writes in *Capital*, citing Hegel.

i.e. even in the sphere of application, it is closely connected with a definite circle of development. [28]

In any event the riddle, originating as a method of testing priests, has permeated all varieties of religious cults, right up to the present. And to an equal degree, it has steadfastly remained in the plot outline of the most popular literary forms and genres.

From the priest's riddle, the tradition of asking riddles runs through countless plots.

Their theme is always the same. In the process of the transition from riddle to solution, there is reproduced the same cultural-historical shift which mankind made when passing from the stage of pre-logical thought to logical thought—that same shift, which, eternally repeating, is accomplished anew by each generation in the development of each individual human consciousness.

This is the pervading and sole plot throughout the wealth of contemporary novels with a riddle—detective novels.

Hence, their amazing efficacy.

For any detective novel, regardless of its story, is for every reader, above all, a novel about himself: about what happened to the reader as a human individual in general; as an individual developing from a child into an adult; as a living being who experiences continuous transitions 'there and back', from layer to layer of consciousness.

That is how the circle of the 'riddle' is drawn: from the riddle of a mystery to the 'mystery-story'—the detective story.

But let us return to our series of examples of what we call 'metonymy in plot'.

Let us briefly enumerate them without going into detail.

Here directly belongs the case where a 'transfer in contiguity', characteristic for the method of metonymy, occurs in fully personified form, as a transfer from one person to a person standing next to him.

In the first example, we had a transfer of action to action: 'seeing through glasses—reading through glasses'; in the second, from one source of action to another source (in contiguity): a burn from nitric acid to an imagined bite from teeth; in the third example: a substitution of a genuine cause for action by a fictitious cause, using the same persuasiveness of this action (crying) for both causes (the broken pitcher—the dead husband).

A case of an actual transfer from one person to another, as a plot situation, occurs in various ways.

Motivated by fantasy, for example:

E. T. A. Hoffmann's 'Klein Zaches' [Little Zack].

This little freak, shortchanged by God in every respect, is endowed with an amazing quality as compensation by a kind fairy:

Whenever something good is done, or thought up, or said in his presence by a 'bystander', some character contiguous with him—it is attributed by those present to Little Zack.

This is the initial plot situation from which a great variety of plot threads is then woven.

And here is the very same plot situation transferred from the conditions of a-logical fantasy (I would say pre-logical fantasy) to completely real conditions:

Lion Feuchtwanger's *Die hässliche Herzogin Margarete Maultasch*.[29] Here, all the judicious policies of state of the deformed margravine, known by the ringing nickname of 'Maultasch' [sack-mouth], are credited to her shallow and frivolous rival, who is distinguished by great beauty and who enjoys the love of the people.

(The motivation for a pre-logical situation with a metonymical transfer is served here by the 'a-logism' of mass popular opinion, which emotionally attributes everything good to their beloved heroine.)

••

It is possible to cite two more examples with a plot trick absolutely identical to that of Shibarsha and Rhampsinitus, with analogous cunning, but which belong to an entirely different epoch and stage of genre literature—the purest stage in terms of its inner link with the norms of the sensuous stage of thought. We outlined it quite recently.

It is the detective story.

I am writing during the evacuation. Far away in the heart of Asia. In the Kazakh city of Alma-Ata.

And though I am set up fairly comfortably, life on my writing desk is a bit crowded and cramped. It sags under a pile of notes on innumerable and just-begun investigations of various problems, from which I tear off these pieces of meat.

It is piled high with countless script notes and shot sketches for *Ivan the Terrible*, which has just entered production.

Sometimes a necktie snakes among them, discarded in a moment of inspiration.

Sometimes—a collar crumpled into a ball.

Less often, socks can be found.

But then very often—traces of hastily eaten food.

Sometimes a drop of some greasy substance is stuck inside a manuscript.

And this morning, I was horrified to discover that several sheets of freshly cut paper were soiled in one corner by stains from this 'precious and nourishing substance', as Buffon would have said had he been writing, not about horses and rats, but about 'Russian butter'.

I cannot stand such disorder when it comes to paper.

And therefore, quickly grab my large scissors and clip off the damaged corners of paper

(According to Anatole France, it is scissors and glue, and not the traditional pen, that are the true emblems of the writer's craft. At one time, I took great joy in this apparent community of the methods of literature and montage.)

Paper with clipped corners takes on an incorrect form.

A 'wrong shape', as they would say in England.

But wait! 'The Wrong Shape' is the name of one of Chesterton's stories about Father Brown![30]

In this story we find the most interesting paraphrase of what Shibarsha did.

Especially interesting because here we have the next stage after Shibarsha and Rhampsinitus.

The stage at which the connection with the initial situational determinant is less obvious.

If, from the formula of the de-individualization and dissolution (diffusion) of the individual 'back to' the undivided 'collective', full apparentness is distinctly preserved in the examples of Shibarsha and Rhampsinitus (all real characters are made up and shaved identically), then here we have the next step: only the 'principle of unification' remains, as a means of 'slipping out' of the world of responsibility into an earlier world, unconstrained by codes of spontaneity.

The continuity of the line is less obvious—people are replaced by objects. But the formula is the same.

But here is the story itself.

It is about the murder of a fantasy writer, Leonard Quinton.

At first it appears to have been suicide.

A white sheet of paper lies on the writer's desk. On it is written in black and white:

'I die by my own hand.'[31]

Everyone is naturally satisfied with this self-confession.

And only Father Brown is dissatisfied with this explanation.

He scrutinizes the paper. ('Father Brown seemed to be studying the paper more than the corpse.')

He is attracted, not by the content of the words, but by that on which the content are embodied—the paper.

And again, not by the paper itself, but only its outward and visible shape.

The shape is wrong.

According to Father Brown—wickedly wrong.

Before this, as always with Chesterton, there had been conversations and arguments on the same theme from a philosophically abstract point of view. They spoke of mean shapes, of the fact that evil and treacherous shapes and designs are often seen in Oriental art under the intoxicating fascination of colours. ('I have seen wicked things in a Turkey carpet... They are letters and symbols in a language I don't know; but I know they stand for evil words... The lines go wrong on purpose—like serpents doubling to escape.)

There are also discussions about the cunning and treacherous shape of a crooked dagger (which lacks the straight point of a spear). It is this dagger that will later be used to commit the murder.

Step by step, the favourite atmosphere of ominous mystery is created, always associated by Chesterton with cultures, philosophies and teachings that stand in opposition to Catholicism (theosophy, atheism, sun-worship—here the religions of the Orient).

Step by step, a shift is produced in the reader towards reading phenomena in terms of the objects or representations which accompany their shape or appearance, but not their content or meaning; i.e. a reorganization towards the so-called physiognomical—directly sensuous perception.

This stage of the development of the action is always given great attention in the best detective stories. The point is not simply to create an atmosphere of mystery, but to totally submerge the reader in the category of imagistic and sensuous thought, without which he cannot endure the keen delight of the passage to the shining edifice of higher intellectual forms, to which the brilliant detective, possessing the wisdom of the higher layers of consciousness, leads him by the hand.

This part of novels is, for the main theme of the novel or story—its refused part.

Incidentally, the very mysteriousness of the atmosphere is created in such a way that the reader is led to this harmony by the characters' conversations (the most widespread device, used here in the introductory part), or else there is an accumulation of conditions or apparently coincidental circumstances, *which conform to the norms of the laws of the primary ideas.* (For example, the dog that howls at the moment of a murder taking place elsewhere, which underlies 'The Oracle of the Dog'[32]—one of the cleverest stories in *The Incredulity of Father Brown*—and which, for all its transcendental appearances, actually has a completely logical solution!)

It is entirely natural that upon perceiving them, the reader is involuntarily drawn into the circle of ideas, characteristic of this thinking.

With Chesterton, this is usually connected with one of the mysterious spiritualistic powers of Catholicism, and the criminal episode serves as a king of extended play of metaphor on an abstract theological thesis. (For example the story, 'The Hammer of God',[33] which tells of a hammer from heaven that strikes down a sinner, but then it turns out that the villain is killed by an actual hammer, thrown by his brother from the parapet of a church tower.)

This device contains a well-known, innately English tradition.

Kipling does a similar thing in *Kim*.

With the only difference that, in contrast to Chesterton, where these elements mutually penetrate each other, with Kipling the theme of the mystical mystery and the theme of criminal-spy mysteries run together in parallel.

Of course, only the great writing skill of a Chesterton is capable of creating in the poetic cogency of the process of a story the grippingness achieved by him of situations woven upon such a primitive—but therefore so effective—foundation.

The schema is incredibly effective, but because of its simplicity and primacy, it demands an especially skillful application to keep from falling into a 'cardboard' cheapness.

And yet Chesterton always preserves beyond the story the aftertaste of a 'parable', i.e. a certain shadow of doubt—that in spite of the simple explanation of the abstract, divine side of his stories, the mysterious force of a divine being exists all the same.

In this respect, his method recalls a well-known, or perhaps not-so-well-known, tale.

(The anecdote about the bottle of Lourdes water in Lucien Fabre's *Le Rire et les rieurs*.)[34]

There too, an atmosphere of miraculousness is created by a coincidence devised in accordance with the formula by which early thought conceives of the occurrence of events and the laws of nature. This confluence of circumstances convinces the reader of his feelings. And the guiding stimulus of the articulated idea is sufficient to cause this feeling to take shape in the desired direction—as a certain belief in otherworldliness.

I analyse this problem in great detail in my unpublished article, 'A Chapter on Dostoyevsky', where I examine how this sense of fate and mystery is formed by means of the intentional structuring of situation according to a law, such as that of the trope.[35] (In the case analysed, through a comparison of a story by Balzac which inspired Dostoyevsky, with the result of its inspiration—*The Brothers Karamazov*. And further, why this sense of Fate is present in Balzac, but not in Dostoyevsky, and why he [Dostoyevsky] specially writes 'judicial error' and not a 'fatal' error. The play of words on the theme 'judicial'—which could be read as an error of the court, as well as an error of . . . Destiny[36]—I, of course, avoid, dealing instead with the question of the inappropriateness of the image of Fate in Dostoyevsky's system of ideas.)

But Leonard Quinton's abandoned body, forgotten somewhere way back in the preceding pages, has meanwhile grown cold.

We left him just as Father Brown had raised to his nose the sheet of paper on which a confession of suicide was written in the inimitable handwriting of the unfortunate writer.

At that instant, lightning illuminates him, and in the ensuing darkness, amidst peals of thunder, the voice of the priest announces to his interlocutor: 'Doctor, this paper is the wrong shape.'[37]

(As we see, the forces of nature coincide with the illuminations and significance of the shrewd priest's utterance.

It is curious to recall that this kind of comparison of events, fusing in perception a coincidence of circumstances, as if at the will of a super-sensuous higher being, underlies one of the most beloved 'gags' of Chaplin. A great lover of performing 'theatre for oneself' or for two or three friends—outside films as well.

Chaplin loves to carry on a blasphemous dialogue in a thunderstorm, amidst the clapping of thunder and lilac, phosphorescent flashes of lightning—a challenge to the forces of nature and the Higher Beings. The roaring rebukes of the forces of nature in response to the Byronic attacks hurled against them by Chaplin, satirizing a tragic actor, are wonderful. And the sheen of his grey hair, illuminated by the lightning, is simply majestic.

It is interesting that the method is the same. And the semi-comicality of the effect results, as always, from a perception of a connection between these wholly absolute phenomena, with the simultaneous awareness of the fact that they are in no way connected with each other.)

The doctor points out to the priest that this was one of Quinton's peculiarities, and that all his paper had the same clipped corners.

He shows him a stack of paper.

Father Brown finds two more sheets with the same irregular shape.

So there are twenty-three of them in all.

But, the attentive Father Brown finds only twenty-two clipped corners!

'Quinton never did commit suicide,' is Brown's final conclusion.[38]

He has figured out the mystery.

A letter from the doctor, who turns out to be the murderer, introduces the final details of the mechanics of the murder which Father Brown has solved.

The sentence: 'I die by my own hand'—was by no means a dying confession.

These words, written at the top of a white sheet of paper, were a line from a novel by Quinton about the conquest of India. (Note the transfer from the category of action to the category of imagination.)

The doctor, who loved Quinton's wife with a criminal passion, is seduced by this opportunity to settle accounts with his lucky rival with impunity. What stands between him and this opportunity?

A few paltry quotation marks, framing a sentence.

Quotation marks cut off, a line transferred from a fragment of a novel, turn into a dying confession of its author—a supposed suicide.

The result is a piece of paper in the wrong shape.

In order to hide it, the isolated sheet with the peculiar shape is reburied in a stack of twenty-two sheets, all cut the same way by the murderer!

Another example from Chesterton might serve as a transitional link between Shibarsha and Rhampsinitus to Chesterton and Ellery Queen.

From living beings to inanimate objects by means of dead people.

I am thinking of the story about General Sir Arthur St Clare, who suffered defeat at the Battle of Black River in Brazil.

Little Father Brown discloses this story to his friend Flambeau while sitting by a tomb—a monument to this commander.

While solving the mystery of this defeat, Father Brown asks:

'Where does a wise man hide a leaf? In the forest. But what does he do if there is no forest?'

'Well, well,' cried Flambeau irritably, 'what does he do?'

'He grows a forest to hide it in.'[39]

Later, step by step, it is revealed that the general needed to kill a Major Murray, who had learned that he was a traitor.

The general murders the major and has to hide the body.

Again the priest asks:

'Where would a wise man hide a leaf? In the forest.'

The other did not answer.

'If there were no forest, he would make a forest. And if wished to hide a dead leaf, he would make a dead forest.'

There was still no reply, and the priest added still more mildly and quietly:

'And if a man had to hide a dead body, he would make a field of dead bodies to hide it in.'

And that is what later turns out to have happened.

The general actually did murder the major.

In doing so, however, he broke the end of his sword.

The tip of the sword remained in the body.

The general leads a head-on attack (in a way that benefits the enemy to whom he had sold out) and buries the corpse he needed to hide in the sea of bodies. ('In twenty minutes eight hundred English soldiers were marching down to their death.')

But a third example along the same line is perhaps even more colourful than the preceding ones.

It is a detective novel by Ellery Queen, a writer completely unknown in our country.

It is called *The Chinese Orange Mystery*.[40]

The title itself contains the whole intrigue. And the whole key to the detective method as well.

The point is that it contains a 'play on words'—i.e. a double reading. Literally, 'Chinese orange' signifies 'an orange from China', but figuratively, it signifies a particular shade of the colour orange (like 'Prussian blue').

In the novel itself, this term has yet a second additional figurative meaning—it is the term for a certain extremely rare and unique Chinese postage stamp, which is orange in colour.

Only one copy of this incredibly valuable stamp exists, and the entire novel is built around its theft and a related murder.

The Chinese oranges—in the non-figurative sense (and not in the sense of public officials!)[41]—that systematically surface in the novel, serve to systematically distract attention in false directions.

I am referring here to the basic trick by which the fundamental piece of evidence is cunningly concealed—the picture of the setting in which the body is found.

(Incidentally, this novel serves as a model of those novels in which tradition is inverted. Thus here the basic mystery is not who *committed* the murder, but who *was murdered*—this strange 'Mr. Nobody from Nowhere'.)

The method of such an inverted solution also nests quite deeply—directly in the primal 'ambivalence'.

And it settles as a solid source of such devices of form as double entendre and word play, or in the rudiments of literature from the child's simple palindrome to specific forms of novels: the cited example of Ellery Queen, or stories of the type that make up R. Austin Freeman's collection, *The Singing Bone*.[42]

If the traditional pattern is here [in Queen] *inverted* in relation to the customary vehicle of the mystery (the murdered—in place of the murderer), then there [in Freeman] it is the sequence of the process of unravelling the mystery that is inverted.

The details of the crime and the identity of the criminal are described at the beginning, and then the process by which they were solved by the detective (Dr Thorndyke)...

And with the magnificence of a first-class master, Ellery Queen uses for his false leads all the figurative psychological reversals, in order to divert attention from the true reason for the situational reversal demanded by his plot. Thus is China entangled in the affair—that treasure-house of models of early thought. In all other respects, the novel develops in the classical fashion, with superb use of the traits of precisely this backward, primal psychology ('backward' in English means both reversed and the past), in both the psychology of his characters, whom the author so successfully catches on this rod, and of his readers.

But then what at last is this novel about?

Step by step he leads the reader with a steady hand for 300 pages towards an unravelling of the basic trick.

But even to the exposition itself, he leads the reader along the same path, from the vaguely understated, imagistic, and allegorical to the fact itself:

The room where the crime was committed:

> The room looked as if some giant hand [N.B.—S.M.E.] had plucked it bodily from the building, shaken it like a dice-cup, and flung it back. At first glance it seemed in a state of utter confusion. All the furniture had been moved. There was something wrong with the pictures on the wall. The rug looked odd. The chairs, the table, everything . . .
>
> There was primarily an impression of ruthless havoc, of furious dismantlement . . . (pp. 33—4)

The body of a stout, bald, middle-aged man is found in the room (the same 'Mr. Nobody from Nowhere', around whom the drama revolves).

As is customary, a physician arrives.

An examination of the body is made.

And the strangeness of the event is first articulated by the doctor:

'*He's got all his clothes on backwards!* . . . His coat is on as if he'd got into it the wrong way, as if somebody held it open facing him and he wriggled into the sleeves and then buttoned himself up the back.' (pp. 40—1)

More follows:

The pervading impression of unreality persisted. [N.B.—S.M.E.] Not only was the dead man's coat on backwards, but his trousers were inverted and buttoned up behind as well. As were his white madras shirt and vest. His narrow stiff collar similarly was turned about, clamped with a shiny gold collar-button at the nape. His undergarments apparently exhibited the same baffling inversion. Of all his clothing only his shoes remained in the orthodox position. (p. 42)

Then the next description of the room completes the picture of the riddle.

An African shield hangs on the wall.

Their attention is drawn to it because the two real spears which had been used in the murder had been wrenched from behind it.

The shield also proves to be inverted (all of chapter three is entitled 'The Topsy-Turvy Murder').

The way it looks elicits a passing remark from the querulous junior detective (even his surname is querulous—Brummer, which in German means 'grumbler'), concerning the nonsensical picture of the murder:

'There's no rhyme or reason to it.' (p. 46)

This is a popular expression in English, meaning nonsense.

When one encounters something absurd, one says it has no rhyme or reason—i.e. a non-coordination of form (rhyme) and content (meaning).

The remark is picked up by the king of the detectives by the name of Queen:

'Rhyme and reason. Exactly . . . That's exactly it. It stuck in my craw from the moment I walked on to this fantastic scene. Rhyme! Rhyme! There's rhyme here that utterly defies analysis, that staggers the imagination.' [N.B. Diffuseness resists analysis. Diffuseness triggered by rhyme—by 'rhythmical repetition'.—S.M.E.] 'If there were no rhyme I should be pleased, very pleased. But rhyme—[one could say co-ordination in repetitions—S.M.E.] there's so much of it, it's so complete and so perfect, that I doubt whether there has ever been a more striking example of it in the whole history of logic!' (p. 45)

Step by step, Queen impresses his idea on the other participants in the scene.

It turns out that the whole setting is also 'in rhyme with the unusual manner in which the deceased is dressed'.

> 'Bookcases? . . . Why, they're turned around to face the walls, Mr Queen.'
>
> 'How about the rug?'
>
> 'It's been turned over, Mr Queen.'
>
> 'And the pictures on the walls?' (p. 46)

Everything turns out to be inverted.

The table with its drawers turned towards the wall, the grandfather clock with its face turned there as well. The same with the deep, comfortable armchairs. And the table lamps, turned upside-down with their bases in the air.

It becomes clear that the furniture and everything else of a movable nature have all been inverted to an equal degree, turned around, turned 'backwards'.

'There's rhyme here that will write detectival history when this case is solved—if it ever is. Everything is backwards! Everything . . . There's your *rhyme*. But how . . . about the *reason*?' (p. 48)

(It is amusing to note that there also takes place here an extension of a concept from the domain of language—rhyme—to objects and the state of objects: the inverted collar rhymes with the inverted rug, the inverted pants with the upside-down lamp. But this, of course, is in the form of a play on words, for the very term, 'rhyme', stands for a broader meaning—'correspondence'.)

Searches are made.

On page 85, the timid sinologist, Miss Temple, formulates what is troubling Mr Queen.

'You mean, Mr Queen, that there's something about the crime, or some one connected with the crime, that possesses *a backward significance*? [i.e. literally—'a meaning lying behind something'—S.M.E.] That some one turned everything backwards *to point to* something backwards about some one, if I make myself clear?' . . .

'It *is* esoteric,' she murmured, 'but then in China you come to accept queer, queer things.'

(N.B. The line of the unusual, the esoteric, the unreal, is constantly being developed.)

Miss Temple suggests interpreting this inversion of objects as a metaphor being expressed in inverted furniture, rugs, bookcases, and pictures.

This is a typical detective-story 'false trail':

an imagistic reading of the evidence, and not in terms of its meaning.

It is presented here in completely bare form. (It is needed so that this line of reasoning drawn by Miss Temple will prevent Mr Queen from arriving at the correct solution right away, even once the question has started to become clear to him.)

Starting on page 108, China enters the picture more strongly. Again with a superficial play on words typical of the Anglo Saxon *calembour* [pun] of the lowest sort—the so-called 'pun'.

The Anglo-Saxons' passion for this is revealed in a charming story about a home for aged wits, where senile old men amuse themselves with an unending game—a play on the double meaning of words. The more ridiculous, base and far-fetched, the funnier the fruits of their wit.

But for this lowest type of word play, primitiveness is their highest virtue. At any rate, thus writes Charles Lamb

(1755–1834), who devotes to this question an entire, very witty essay about the fact 'That the Worst Puns Are the Best'.[43]

Miss Temple introduces a series of ideas leading to a Chinese, i.e. an 'imagistic' (and in the given case, an incorrect), interpretation of the circumstances and evidence, in response to Mr Queen's play on words:

'China is a sadly *backward* country.'

Yet another reading of the meaning of the term 'backward'.

This causes Queen to follow false trails later on page 112: might there not be something directly backward in the manners and customs of the Chinese that could serve as an indication to the concealed meaning of the fact that everything is turned inside out? ('How about the Chinese theatre? Anything backwards there? . . . And how about Chinese oranges?')

The meaning of this manipulation lies not at all in the fact of the inversion itself, as we shall see below, and that is why this *visible side* of the fact is constantly accented throughout the novel, intentionally falsely accented—in order to better conceal its *essence*.

Even the selection of the peculiarities of Chinese behaviour described by Miss Temple, furthers the line of thought precisely in this direction.

Here is a typical example:

It is customary to pay bills twice a year.

That makes it very convenient for debtors.

They simply go into hiding on these days (one of which is New Year's Eve), and the creditors have no luck when they knock on their doors.

But the poor creditors find a way out of this situation

On New Year's Day, they keep knocking on the debtors' doors, while carrying a lighted lantern.

Ellery stared: 'Why the lighted lantern?'

Miss Temple explains: 'The lighted lantern carried by the creditor is supposed to prove that it is not New Year's Day at all, when, according to custom they are no longer allowed to collect money, but that it is still New Year's Eve, when, according to the same custom, they must be paid.

(In itself, 'custom' is a marvellous illustration of the norms of pre-logical thought. From a part—the lighted lantern—is imagined the whole: the night before! The same mechanism as in sympathetic magic, examples of which we cited earlier.)[44]

In any event, all these ideas about China achieve their purpose.

And only the reader is attuned to an imagistic, and not a logical interpretation of the details of the event. Even Ellery Queen himself admits that, as a result of all this, he was mistaken in supposing that the inversion of the objects *points out* something concerning the perpetrators of the crime, whereas in fact the true purpose of the inverted things was *to conceal* something connected with the perpetrators of the drama,

i.e. the essential thing was not at all the visible side of the fact that everything is inverted, but the fact that indeed *everything* is inverted.

And everything is inverted for the purpose of concealing the one 'key' detail which possessed this fatal mark, which could not be hidden in any way other than the one employed by the criminal in the given case— following the example of Rhampsinitus, Shibarsha and General St Clare.

He had to resort to this traditional method because he did not have at his disposal a necktie.

At this point, of course, I should go on with a protracted digression for many pages, in order to thoroughly enrage the reader.

And then at some point recall:

'Wait a minute! Did I forget to give the solution?'

I'll give it, I'll give it, I'll give it.

The whole secret lies in the fact that the victim was a Catholic priest who had just returned from China, where he had worked as a missionary.

And? And?

And Catholic priests wear stiff collars turned around and with no tie!

The most important thing for the murderer to conceal was the fact that the victim was a priest.

This fact would have helped to reveal the identity of the victim immediately, which inevitably would have explained everything.

The murderer successfully removes the priest's cassock.

But, for total concealment of the victim's profession, he lacks . . . a necktie.

And that is why, instead of inverting the collar, which he cannot fasten for lack of the essential necktie, he reverses everything in the room.

In this way he conceals the exceptionality of the circumstance that only the collar is backwards.

He places everything else on the same level as the position of the collar, and in this way submerges in the non-differentiated general mass of identically rhymed things, that sole piece of evidence which could put the detectives on his trail.

A familiar device.

Incidentally, I recall here one more variation on the same theme—an episode from Abel Gance's film, *Napoleon* [France, 1927], which I cited in my article, 'More Thoughts on Structure'.[45]

There it is used for a different purpose.

But I would prefer that one read the whole context concerning my reason for citing this episode from *Napoleon*.

That reason was the peculiarity of the stylistic treatment of a character from a different film—*Chapayev*.[46]

What we have examined here as a situational and plot condition, is there an element of the method of portrayal and conscious treatment.

We have analysed here the true nature of this device in sufficient detail. The last example gives us the right to consider it the basis not only of form, not only of situation, but also of the methodology of conscious treatment.

NOTES

1 This essay is an extract from *Method*. Although E did
   not date the manuscript, it can tentatively be attributed
   to late February or early March 1944. It was first published as 'O detektive' in *Prikliuchencheskii fil'm: puti i
   poiski* [Adventure Film: Avenues and Research]
   (Moscow: *VNIIK*, 1980), from which Upchurch translated it.

2 Between 1911 and 1913, a total of 32 *Fantômas* novels
   appeared—the creation of Marcel Allain (1885–1969)
   and Pierre Souvestre (1874–1914). Their immense
   popularity led to an immediate film serial based on the
   first five books, *Fantômas* [France, 1913], directed by
   Louis Feuillade (1873–1925). It is probable that
   Feuillade's serial greatly influenced the underworld
   intrigue and *policier* elements in E's first feature film,
   Stachka [The Strike, 1925].

3 *Les Vampires* [France, 1915–16] was another film serial
   directed by Feuillade, this time in nine episodes.

4 The reference is to the Kitai-gorod [Chinatown] dis-
   trict of central Moscow.

5 Subsequent development of the city centre and, in particular, the construction of the Hotel Rossiya, has led to parts of the wall being once again exposed to public view.

6 *La Lanterne* was a weekly paper, specializing in political satire, founded in 1868 by Henri de Rochefort (1831–1913). See *ESW4*, pp. 135, 192, 363, 371–2.

7 See p. 127, n. 7.

8 *Le Cercueil vide* [The Empty Coffin], VOL. 25 of *Fantômas* (Paris: Fayard, 1913).

9 *Un Roi prisonnier de Fantômas* [A King Imprisoned by Fantômas], VOL. 5 of *Fantômas* (Paris: Fayard, 1911).

10 *La Cravate de chanre*, VOL. 31 of *Fantômas* (Paris: Fayard, 1913).

11 Gatchina was actually the site of one of the tsar's summer palaces outside St Peterburg.

12 *Fantômas* (Paris: Fayard, 1911).

13 *La Main coupée* [The Severed Hand], VOL. 10 of *Fantômas* (Paris: Fayard, 1911).

14 The *Fantômas* novel that E is here describing has not been identified.

15 Here E left a gap in the manuscript, which has been filled with the definition from *The Compact Edition of the Oxford English Dictionary* (New York: Oxford University Press, 1971), VOL. 1, p. 1784.

16 A. N. Veselovskii, 'Skazki ob Ivane Groznom' in *Sobranie sochinenii* (Moscow: AN SSSR, 1938), VOL. 16, pp. 156–7.

17 Ibid., p. 157.

18 E is referring to Heine's 'Romanzero', *Rhampsenit*. See: *The Complete Poems of Heinrich Heine* (Hal Draper trans.) (Cambridge, MA: Suhrkamp/Insel, 1982), pp. 563–5.

19 E is mistaken here on several points. He has confused the character of King Rhampsinitus with the unnamed thief of the same legends. Second, the situation he describes here does not belong to the legend of Rhampsinitus, but to a similar legend of the Roman Emperor Philip, which is also recounted by Veselovsky (VOL. 16, p. 188). It is surprising that E does not cite the tale of 'Rhampsinitus and the Thief', as told by Herodotus and also recounted by Veselovsky: this describes how the thief uses the dead man's arm to avoid capture, thus bearing a close resemblance to the scene in *Fantômas* described by E earlier. See: Herodotus, *The Histories* (Harmondsworth: Penguin, 1972), p. 177.

20 Elsewhere in *Method*, E analyses *The Merchant of Venice* in greater detail.

21 A reference to the play *Gore ot uma* [Woe from Wit, 1822–24] by Alexander S. Griboyedov (1794–1829).

22 A reference to the scene in Tolstoy's *War and Peace* that E analysed in *Direction* (*IP4*, p. 472).

23 *IP4*, pp. 465–6.

24 See p. 63, n. 9.

25 Friedrich Engels, *Socialism: Utopian and Scientific*, *Selected Works*, VOL. 2 (Moscow: Progress Publishers), p. 121.

26 E's source has not been identified.

27 Cited in: H. S. Chamberlain, *Goethe* (Munich: Bruckmann, 1912), p. 386.

28 E probably has the following passage from Hegel cited by Marx:

> Reason is just as cunning as she is powerful. Her cunning consists principally in her mediating activity, which, by causing objects to act and re-act on each other in accordance with their own nature, in this way, without any direct interference in the process, carries out reason's intentions.

[Karl Marx, *Capital*: *A Critique of Political Economy*, VOL 3 (Friedrich Engels ed., Samuel Moore and Edward Aveling trans) (New York: International Publishers, 1967), p. 175.]

29 Published in English as *The Ugly Duchess* (W. and E. Muir trans) (London: Secker, 1927).

30 G. K. Chesterton, 'The Wrong Shape' in *The Innocence of Father Brown* (New York: Penguin, 1950[1911]).

31 The quotations are from ibid., pp. 141, 142 and 135.

32 G. K. Chesterton, 'The Oracle of the Dog' in *The Incredulity of Father Brown* (New York: Penguin, 1958[1926]).

33 In *The Innocence of Father Brown*.

34 L. Fabre, *Le Rire et les rieurs* [Laughter and Those Who Laugh] (Paris: Gallimard, 1929).

35 Portions of E's article 'A Chapter on Dostoyevsky', in which he compares *The Brothers Karamazov* with Balzac's story 'L'Auberge rouge' [1831], were translated for the first time in: N. M. Lary, *Dostoevsky and Soviet*

Film: *Visions of Demonic Realism* (Ithaca, NY: Cornell University Press, 1986), pp. 255–64.

36 All three words share the same root in Russian: *sudebnyi* [judicial], *sud* [court], *sudba* [destiny].

37 Chesterton, 'The Wrong Shape', p. 142.

38 Chesterton, 'The Wrong Shape', p. 147.

39 G. K. Chesterton, 'The Sign of the Broken Sword' in *The Innocence of Father Brown*. The quotations are from pp. 219, 226 and 229.

40 Ellery Queen, *The Chinese Orange Mystery* (New York: Stokes, 1934). Page numbers for quotations are given in the text.

41 E translates the title of the novel as *Taina kitaiskogo mandarina* [The Mystery of the Chinese *Mandarin*], which affords him the possibility of this additional word play.

42 R. Austin Freeman, *The Singing Bone* (New York: Dodd, Mead, 1923).

43 Charles Lamb, 'That the Worst Puns Are the Best' ('Popular Fallacies', IX) in *The Life and Works of Charles Lamb*, VOL. 2: *The Last Essays of Elia* (London: Macmillan, 1899), pp. 211–14.

44 *NIN*, p. 379–82.

45 *FEL*, pp. 92–108.

46 *Chapayev*: see above, p. 68, n. 30. The film was the subject of E's November 1934 article 'At Last!', *ESW1*, pp. 296–300, and is mentioned several times in the articles in *ESW3*.

LECTURES ON LITERATURE[1]
[TRAGEDY AND COMEDY IN PLOT]

Individual problems of art resemble each other.

In Shakespeare's *Richard III*, there is an extraordinarily expressive confession of love.

Let's see how this situation might develop into other situations—that is, what the result will be when improbable and exceptional elements start to diminish or intensify.

Richard III is a work situated somewhere on the verge of hyperbole.

How much further would the tragedy and its situations have to go before exceeding the bounds of common sense, and what is required to soften the harshness of the drama?

What does the situation of Richard III standing over the murdered corpse while confessing his love to the widow remind us of?

The situation of Don Juan and Donna Anna, of course.

I've long been interested in the connection of this scene in *Richard III* with legends of Don Juan.[2] It's interesting that other scenes in *Richard III* also recall *Don Juan*.

It is up to literary historians to refine and establish the deeper connections, and to identify corresponding mythological analogies and premises.

What is the basic, dramaturgical difference between the similar scenes in *Richard III* and *Don Juan*? There is a psychological difference in the relationship of the characters. The heroine in *Don Juan* doesn't know that he killed her father, and she only learns it at the height of his confession of love. The situation in *Richard III* is different. Lady Anne knows from the very beginning that Richard is the murderer. But, in spite of this, she controls her temper. This accounts for the seemingly greater cogency of the scene in *Don Juan* than the scene in *Richard III*.

Consequently, the difference between these analogous situations lies in the fact that in *Richard III*, we are shown a sudden change from one emotion to its direct opposite. And in a very emphasised form. The spectator witnesses this change from its beginning to its end. Here we see an unmistakable stylistic pointer to the passion from which this scene must proceed, to its inner degree of intensity.

In order for the change of the emotion to its antithesis to be felt as persuasive, a task of incredibly complex intensity and maximum tension is required.

If we sketch in our minds the levels of tension in *Don Juan* and *Richard III*, we see that the intensity in Shakespeare's tragedy is one step higher. Can we guess the next step above Richard? Can Richard's emotion be pushed any further in intensity?

There is a work by a highly respected author, whose situation can be formulated in a few words: a man murdered a woman's husband, confessed his love to the wife, and she agreed to live with him. A man murders a husband and marries the wife, but where is this even more horrible than in *Richard III*?

In *Oedipus*.

This is the next step in psychological intensity after *Richard III*.

Oedipus is more horrible than Richard because he kills his own father and marries his own mother—that is, an analogous situation taken in a different degree. This is the next point along the line of horrors.

There also exists in world literature a comical combination of this same theme. It is sufficient to recall the 'Widow of Ephesus' fragment in Petronius' *Satyricon*. This is one of the classic stories. So there are various degrees of one and the same situation, there are variations on one and the same theme with a different degree of emphasis.

A very interesting question arises: might not the connection here between these three plots be deeper than it appears at first glance? Could *Richard III* and later, *Don Juan*, be a modification of the situation in *Oedipus* ?

If we look at *Richard III*, we'll no doubt discover in this situation a connection with an ancient practice of mankind. In his aesthetic treatise, *The Analysis of Beauty*, the artist Hogarth writes that each work of art contains a permeating artistic law.

Everything is constructed upon this law; this law is repeated in every detail, no matter how trifling. Hogarth writes that the fascination, the gripping impression from a true work of art must be attributed to the survival of the hunting stage of consciousness.[3] The satisfaction received by the mind and senses of a man who pursues the permeating law in a work of art, is analogous to the emotion felt by a full-blooded Englishman hunting a fox. I've given a paradoxical example and personally do not believe that the captivating effect of repetitions and laws in art is based on a survival of the hunting period in human consciousness. But the very possibility of such an idea is perfectly understandable. It gives a sense of the fact that earlier, past experience plays a very large role in the phenomenon of art.

When reading the scenes of Richard III's and Anne's confession of love, we are not revolted. The very opposite: each of us feels that if he were in Anne's place, he would react the same as she. The reason is that Shakespeare portrays Richard not on a negative level, but as a man with an awesome, tremendous strength of spirit.

We have here, essentially, a reversal of an ancient practice of human society from the period when girls of neighbouring tribes were abducted from their parents, violently kidnapped, and then paid for by bride-money, a dowry. A form of dowries still exists. The true nature of the situation is based on a very ancient practice.

When you think about these feelings, you understand that this kind of thing can be achieved in a modern work only when the condition within the drama recalls some former condition from antiquity. A gripping work can never be achieved unless it is created by the artist's entire organism, by all his thoughts and feelings. The theme of a work must inflame; in developing a theme, the very highest and deepest layers of consciousness must be tapped. Only when creative rapture penetrates all layers of the artist's brain, down to his animal-emotional layers, can a work of art truly captivate the reader.

[POLYGENRISM]

'Polygenrism' should be taken as a very relative term. It can be present within the fabric of work; polygenrism can grow between episodes for the purpose of preserving their unity. Finally, polygenrism can set off individual episodes, and then the result is not a picture, but a suite of individual shots. There is also unconscious polygenrism, which is neither realised nor felt by its own author. Then polygenrism contradicts the scene's character. The resulting scenes are simply unmoving.

If an author borrows a device from another genre, a different poetics completely out of place—it would be the same as if, during a lecture, I began singing an operatic recitative for no reason whatsoever. There are elements of polygenrism in the removal of pathos from a work. On one hand, this involves the assembly of a pathetic-rhythmical construction, and then the ironic-everyday level; and both of these levels—the pathetic and the everyday—are placed in such interrelations that one cancels out the other. The pathos of the work disappears.

What happens in short stories?

They are often written in a different genre, but if you compile them into one long work, certain scenes of such work will acquire the character of short stories. Take *The Pickwick Papers* with its inserted short stories. These inserted short stories ultimately result in an integral novel, but nuances are still preserved.

A Thousand and One Nights is constructed according to the same principle. This is an early form of literature. Later new forms arrive, but the characteristics of actions and heroes remain for a long time at the level of old forms. We know that whenever a new character appears in novels, something changes in the action, language, or style.

In modern literature, an individual intonation must be found for each element of the work.

But there was time when the intonation was a measure of the style of the epoch.

Whenever we switch to imagistic speech in moments of the greatest poetic intensity, we are appealing to a semantic category, when the only possible way of speaking is imagistically.

What I mean is this: metaphoric speech can be used when no other speech yet exists. Take, for example, Chinese philosophy. It is all written in verse, as poetic descriptions. Heine writes well about this in regard to the Indians. I don't remember the exact quote. I can only say that the

German poet believes the long poems of the Indians to be historical chronicles and that the key to decoding their facts has been lost. These poems are so floridly worded, one wants to re-close all the flowers. When, instead of the 'sun', people say the 'flaming ball that comes up in the morning', they speak that way not from mannerism, but because they lack a corresponding designation for the object, in this case the sun. It's easy to retrace this fact in the phenomenon of the sun, but there are many other phenomena expressed in the same form, and what they designate is not known. The connection has been lost.

Heine wrote superbly about this. Whenever you need to use a poetic metaphor, image, etc., you are turning to the categories of the ancient art of poetry.

In studying the history of art, we see that any epoch in which thinking was at the level of today's poetic symbols, also expressed itself symbolically, in imagery and metaphor in works of literature. One need only recall Firdousi and Ossetian poetry.[4]

The same can be said of Transcaucasian toasts and the speeches of their toasts and the speeches of their toast-masters.

[THE GROTESQUE]

Upon what is the fascination of the grotesque constructed?

It is constructed upon unclosed lines.

What is the basic motif of the grotesque?

The combination of reality and fantasy, the combination of two opposite levels.

Take Hoffmann's *Der goldne Topf.*[5] Its heroine is an apple seller. But she also happens to be a witch. Lindhorst is an old archivist, but by night—a glowing salamander.

Hoffmann's metamorphoses occur with characters not as a normal transformation.

When he is an archivist, Lindhorst wears a smock that suggests he is a glowing salamander.

When Lindhorst turns into a glowing salamander, his clothes retain the traces of an archivist.

These elements of an artificial reduction of fantasy and reality also create the specifics that are unique to the grotesque.

A non-reduction of levels, an absence of synthesis, are also a mark of the grotesque.

Elements which are usually merged and synthesised are present in the grotesque without fusing together.

If these elements were united, we would have a work of a different order, not the grotesque.

In the case of Hoffmann, the grotesque use of fantasy and reality is distinctly clear. The material and non-material levels are present not as a unity, which shows first one side and then the other, but the opposite: there is a creeping of one level into the other and an emphasised collision of the real and the unreal. This too distinguishes the grotesque.

We know that a unity of the material and non-material is present and exists in nature. That is a non-grotesque unity. But when material and non-material elements are artificially detached from each other, and then deliberately rejoined, run into each other as a collision, then an effect arises which is specific to the grotesque.

Here is the difference between Gogol and Hoffmann: Hoffmann would stick 'The Nose' in *Evenings on a Farm near Dikanka*, but Gogol divides his works up into the fantastic, as 'The Nose' is to a certain extent, and the everyday. Elements present in his 'Petersburg Tales' are not to be found in *Dead Souls*. But Hoffmann bring these two levels together. That is the basic difference between them in terms of the grotesque.

Take Sobakevich. The outline of this character is entirely possible, assembled as he is from individual typical traits. But the degree to which Sobakevich is reworked by Gogol is such that he could never leave the academic edition of Gogol's works and lose himself in a crowd on the streets.

[THE DETECTIVE STORY]

In what way is the detective story good?

In that it is the most effective genre of literature. You cannot tear yourself away from it. It is constructed with means and devices that maximally rivet the reader. The detective story is the most drastic means, the most purified, sharpened construction in a number of similar literatures. It is the genre where the means of influence are bared to the limit.

Usually the thematic, cognitive level of the detective story is very low. Often the detective story lacks an ideological grasp of any kind. Throughout the history of cinema, there have been repeated attempts to put material of the Bolshevik underground in traditional detective story forms. They all failed. When this was tried in the twenties and thirties, the result was not a closing of ranks, but an almost naked constructivism, for a profound, serious content was squeezed into an unserious form.

The detective story is the most naked expression of bourgeois society's fundamental ideas on property.

The entire history of the detective story encompasses the battle over property. On this level, the modifications of detective story material are very interesting. For example, the beginning of the nineteenth century, coinciding with the development and growth of the bourgeoisie, nominates whom as a hero? The adventurer, the criminal: the Count of Monte Cristo and Rocambole;[6] that is, heroes connected with a certain romantic protest and who are therefore noble. Then in the middle or second half of the nineteenth century, who becomes the hero? The inspector who protects property and catches bandits who dare to encroach upon ownership. The centre of gravity here is modified during the nineteenth century, and this is extremely interesting.

One way or another, detective literature is proprietary not only in content, but in its literary goals as well. It is the means of maximum money-making—that is, the desire for a large print run.

Therefore, the selection of the means of influence in the detective story bears the mark of the franc or dollar. The most effective novel will have the largest printing and will bring in the greatest profit. And so under this monetary pressure, there also occurs an absolute purification of devices.

So tightly are they screwed in, they show through. If we know what these devices are, we can quickly make out the plot outline.

Interesting things result in the detective story when the structure of this genre starts to acquire literary material of a superior quality.

Which writers?

Dostoyevsky.

Almost every work by Dostoyevsky is a typical crime novel with an investigation or whatever.

Crime and Punishment and *The Brothers Karamazov* have the outlines of typical crime novels. In terms of their plot development and plot tasks, maximally effective outlines are chosen (and of a deeply serious nature: in *Karamazov*—the murder of one's parents) and placed upon absolutely believable, affective material. Therefore, to read such material and examine it in a comparative analysis, to see how this is done, is extremely interesting.

If you compare a dozen novels of one group with a dozen novels of another, you will always locate the mechanics of the absolute means of influence. You will uncover the key moments from which the action freely develops.

The most interesting thing is that the detective novel is connected with quite ancient material. It operates upon an extremely old and even very low complex. If you compare certain thematic moments between detective novels and mythology or epos, it's not hard to see that a number of concepts from religious-mythological literature have been grafted on to popular literature.

Let's take the most popular situation of all detective novels. A person has died and, incidentally, not just died, but has been resurrected. That is, the character appeared to have died, but in fact he didn't, he continued to function. This is a theme on which religion has speculated for many thousands of years.

It is sufficient to recall Rocambole in *Le Club des valets-de-coeur*,[7] the story of Lord Andrea who is invisible to all, who hides from everyone, and who possesses literally all the traits hitherto enjoyed by God alone. He is omnipresent, omniscient and omnipotent. From London, Lord Andrea controls India and Australia, he has contacts in all corners of the world; that is, we have before us literal copy of the model of an omnipotent God, which has captivated people over the course of many centuries.

Remember that the layout of a scene must be approached not by a creeping path—from the first step and on and on to the end; rather, you must always pick out the points of rest that lie ahead.

You should always know the stations you are headed for.

Edgar Allan Poe, who, as is well known, was the forefather of the detective genre, made a classic statement in this regard. His 'Murders in the Rue Morgue' is one of the first detective stories. Even more interesting is 'The Purloined Letter'. It is more striking and original. Poe's short story is unusual in the way in which a letter is cleverly concealed. It is left in the most conspicuous place.

Conan Doyle appeared considerably later. In Poe, we find the first classical formulas of the detective story. Everything else in this genre comes from Poe.

Poe constructs his plot in a very interesting way, and he is the forefather of the genre with the most complexly constructed plot. In a theoretical article on how to write verse, stories, etc., Poe says that every story should be written from the end; that is, one must establish for oneself an utterly precise composition to which the story is leading, and construct the plot backwards. Of course, this is somewhat of an exaggeration. It's not mandatory to construct from the very end, but to construct, I would say, simultaneously from the beginning and from the end, keeping in mind the middle sections all the while. Then will you have a truly proper correspondence among all the separate parts.

There exists a statement—by Talleyrand,[8] I believe—to the effect that one should never utter one's first thought, because it always corresponds to reality and is always truthful. For Talleyrand's profession, this was in fact true. He was not supposed to ever utter his first thought; Talleyrand's profession was such that the expression of his first thought would have been an inappropriate quality.

An artist is a different matter.

For an artist, it is always important to strengthen the first sensation, the first thought, because it is always a direct response to that which occurs to him.

If you have read the detective novels about Sherlock Holmes, what is the basic conflict here? Between whom?

Between Watson and Holmes.

Watson is the representative of what tendency?

All the evidence points to this man, so he must be the murderer.

But what is Sherlock Holmes's position?

All the evidence points to such-and-such a man, so he can't be the murderer.

Watson and Scotland Yard always work along the line of direct logic.

Sherlock Holmes works not by logic, but by dialectics.

All of you are now in the position of Watson because, when working out your scenes, you are perceiving only what is most simple and apparent, without taking into consideration the attendant circumstances, in particular the perception of the viewer. In real life, if a man needs to exit through a door, he does so. But on the stage, that won't do. On the stage, this must be done in such a way that he thinks about it first and then decides to leave. Only then will it be clear that he left. Legible movement on the stage is not constructed on the basis of formal logic. It must be constructed on dialectics, on the negation of a negation.

[SHAKESPEARE]

Each of Shakespeare's plays turns out to have its own set of images. If it's a line from *Romeo and Juliet*, you won't find an image from *King John*. That work has its own images. It's interesting that in *Richard III*, which deals primarily with the problem of dynastic rule (he kills off all his relatives), the drama takes place on the branches of a genealogical tree. If you look at both *Richard III* and *Henry VI*, which precedes it chronologically, both plays are constructed on a single linguistic image. And the leading imagery is trees, gardens, growth, branches and so forth; that is, elements of a genealogical tree are constantly used for metaphors, similes, and images.

In *Romeo and Juliet*, everything is built on images of light, sunshine, or rays. Every simile, every metaphor comes without fail from the circle of ideas concerning light. But in *Richard III*, which I want to emphasise, it is problems of growth, pruning of branches, overgrowth, a garden overrun by weeds, the choking of one plant by another—this is the complex of imagistic metaphors that Shakespeare uses throughout.

As an image of a man, Macbeth is almost inseparable from Lady Macbeth, because both are mutually dependent on a complex of circumstances. Whenever we say: Lear, Richard, or Othello, we see individual images, but when we recall Macbeth, our impression is that of a complex. Shakespeare's treatment of the image of Macbeth is brilliantly conveyed early in the exposition of the tragedy: recall the witches' sabbath and Macbeth's first appearance.

Fate plays a large role in the development of the plot of *Macbeth*.

Macbeth is weaving of fate into a tragic story; there are even elements of horror in Shakespeare's drama— snakes. The tragic side in general is very pronounced.

Richard III, in contrast to Macbeth, is an openly individual personality. All his schemes and calculations are woven like those of Ostap Bender.[9] It is no accident that

Richard III begins with a monologue. This predetermines the whole course of the drama.

Macbeth is not felt as a separate image, individualised and unrepeatable; he is swept along by a complex of fate throughout the whole story. And this intention of Shakespeare is reflected in the opening structure of the tragedy.

You remember that a forest approaches, and it is said that Macbeth will be killed by a man born not of a woman. It is under this omen, this symbol of the hero's approaching doom, that the exposition of the tragedy unfolds.

There are also a number of demons in *Richard III*. Ghosts appear to the hero and talk to him. But these demons differ from those in *Macbeth*. The ghosts in *Macbeth* are real. In *Macbeth*, it's a matter of metaphor—a forest moves towards Macbeth a man born not of woman will kill him.

Every symbol in *Macbeth* turns out to be something real.

In *Richard*, the ghosts are the voice of his conscience, they are abstracted from his personality and deeds.

Here we see the method of false metaphor.

This method is popularised in detective novels.

In Gaston Leroux's *The Phantom of the Opera*, everything is constructed on false metaphor. The novel contains a number of strange descriptions. When the hero is led through the gallery of the theatre, he is instructed to hold his hand over his face. Without any explanation. The impression given is that this is some kind of ritualistic sign. But then it is revealed to be a very simple matter—the heroes believed that a noose would be thrown around their neck at any moment, but if they walked with their hand held in front of their face, the noose would be thrown over their hand and they could not be strangled.

Gaston Leroux's novel also contains a story of a horrible face without a body that moves along the corridors of the opera house. Then the mystery is explained. It turns out that the horrible face is an old man who catches rats and whose lantern illuminates only his physiognomy.

As you can see, all the elements of the novel are plunged in the darkest mystery, but then it turns out that the action itself could not be more natural.

Take the recent novel, *The Dragon Murder Case*, which is about people who dive into a swimming pool and don't come back up.[10] They are killed while swimming. When a body is pulled from the pool, marks are always found on it which resemble a dragon's claw. When the pool is drained, prints of antediluvian paws are found in the silt. Terrifying assumptions are made. But then it turns out that there was a man in a diving suit sitting on the bottom of the pool who murdered the divers with a hook on the end of his glove. The action is put together as a mysterious story about a man-eating dragon. The explanation of the events is exceedingly simple.

There are elements of a similar construction in *Macbeth*. Here the double meaning of a metaphor is at work: on one hand, the incredible and the mysterious, and on the other—the simplest fact.

The same phenomenon is found in the opening fight scene in *Romeo and Juliet*. This is a quite clearly expressed leitmotif, since all the subsequent events lead up to a fight, a clash of two hostile forces.

But a reverse construction on the very same plot material is also possible. If the whole thing is based, for example, on a quarrel, then the play or novel begins not with the quarrel, but the opposite—with a presentation of extremely friendly relations. But in the final analysis, the compositional result is the same.

Characters are developed from two directions simultaneously: that which is given by the author, and that which arises from the action itself and then throws new light upon the character.

What does the text give us? There is a list of characters and a description: first murderer, second murderer, etc. As in *Macbeth*.

Do you remember the scene of Banquo's murder? If you take the list of characters, there is no identification of the murderers.

It simply says: first, second, third.

There is no description and hardly a role at all: everything is realised in the action. It could be done simply. Make one a bass, another a treble, but that would be an unmotivated device.

Here is a purely speculative conclusion I once drew on this subject.

Sergei Yutkevich and I once designed some sets for *Macbeth*, I believe in 1921. There was a certain 'Polenov House' on the Boulevard Ring [in Moscow] where we worked with the director Tikhonovich.[11]

I had read some of the literature on *Macbeth* and was struck by one particular circumstance—that there are three killers in the murder scene, but only two report it to Macbeth. There is a discrepancy in the number of characters. I thought about it and decided that the third character present at Banquo's murder should be Macbeth himself. Then the other two come to him with their report.

In *King Lear*, Shakespeare links the unity of the state in a poetic figure of speech to an image of a corpse; what image is this tragedy dealing with the destruction of the state built on? Completely on torture, the mutilation of the body, the twisting of arms, the mutilation of the breast, the gouging out of eyes—you remember that gouging out eyes and crushing them underfoot is introduced even in the action, and not only in speech. Of all Shakespeare's tragedies, the most inhuman, in the sense of the treatment of the human body, is *King Lear*.

Radlov once wrote about the reversibility of the endings of Shakespeare's tragedies, comparing the finales of the great English dramatist to O. Henry's twist endings.[12]

Radlov made a great mistake.

Shakespeare's final thematic twist is always prepared for by the contradictions of its development. His action develops towards one side of a contradiction, but towards the end, it rolls towards the other side.

The structure of O. Henry's stories is always a mechanical opposition. His endings result not from contradictions with the theme, but from a situation chosen for contrast. One has to examine but a few of O. Henry's short stories to recognise this device, and to be convinced of its monotony.

O. Henry is very unexpected and fascinating for the first three stories, but by the fourth you already know in advance what's going to happen.

The contradictions in Shakespeare's plays always result from the internal elements of the work. Recall the attitude of Gloucester in *King Lear* to one son and to the other. Despite the abruptness of the change, the character's behaviour is connected with the whole course of the drama, and is therefore internally justified. In this regard, Hegel made a brilliant comment: Gloucester had to become blind in order to see.

Thus, the groundwork for an unexpected ending must be laid in the very structure of the work's development.

NOTES

1 These selected passages from various lectures given by E to his students at VGIK throughout the 1930s and 1940s were first published in the monthly journal *Voprosy literatury* 1 (January 1968). The precise dates of these lectures have not been determined. The titles have been provided by the editors.

2 In *Direction*, E discussed several versions of Don Juan, most notably Molière's *Dom Juan ou le festin de pierre* [Don Juan or the Stone Banquet] and Pushkin's 'little tragedy' *The Stone Guest*. See *IP4*, p. 138.

3 W. Hogarth, *The Analysis of Beauty* (J. Burke ed.) (Oxford: Clarendon Press, 1955), p. 42.

4 Firdousi (*c.*941–1020), a Persian poet, whose major work was *Shahnama*, an epic history of Persia in 60,000 couplets.

5 See *The Selected Writings of E. T. A. Hoffmann* (L. J. Kent and E. C. Knight ed. and trans.) (Chicago: University of Chicago Press, 1969).

6 The Count of Monte Cristo was the hero of a novel by Alexandre Dumas (1802–70). Rocambole was the

central character in a series of twenty-two novels by Pierre-Alexis Ponson du Terrail (1829-71).

7 *Le Club des valets-de-coeur* [The Jack of Hearts Club] was the fourth volume of Ponson du Terrail's Rocambole series.

8 Charles Maurice de Talleyrand-Périgord (1754–1838), French statesman and diplomat.

9 Ostap Bender was the scheming conman featured in two satirical novels, *The Twelve Chairs* [1928] and *The Golden Calf* [1931] by Ilf and Petrov, the joint pen-name of Ilya Ilf (1897–1937) and Evgeni P. Katayev (1903–42).

10 S. S. Van Dine, *The Dragon Murder Case* (New York: Scribner's, 1933).

11 E and Yutkevich were invited by the director V. Tikhonovich to design the sets for *Macbeth* in November 1921. It was produced at the Polenov House of Drama Education, a small theatre used mainly for amateur productions, in April 1922. Among the other peculiarities of their design were highly stylised costumes and a single set in which the whole performance was to be played without a curtain drop. For Yutkevich's recollections of the project, see his English-language article 'Eisenstein, Scene-Painter' in *Eizenshtein: Teatral'nye risunki* [Eisenstein: Theatrical Drawings], (Moscow: Soiuz kinematografistov SSSR, 1970), pp. 9–10, and illustrations 22–3. See also: Y. Barna, *Eisenstein* (Bloomington: Indiana University Press, 1973), p. 58.

12 Sergei E. Radlov (1892–1958), a proponent of psychological and realistic theatre, staged many productions
of Shakespeare's works in the 1930s. The source E
refers to has not been identified.